RAPE FOR PROFIT

Trafficking of Nepali Girls and Women to India's Brothels

Human Rights Watch/Asia

Human Rights Watch
New York • Washington • Los Angeles • London • Brussels

Human Rights Watch/Asia

Human Rights Watch/Asia was established in 1985 to monitor and promote the observance of internationally recognized human rights in Asia. Sidney Jones is the executive director; Mike Jendrzejczyk is the Washington director; Robin Munro is the Hong Kong director; Jeannine Guthrie is NGO Liaison; Dinah PoKempner is Counsel; Zunetta Liddell and Patricia Gossman are research associates; Mark Girouard and Shu-Ju Ada Cheng are Luce fellows; Diana Tai-Feng Cheng and Jennifer Hyman are associates; Mickey Spiegel is a research consultant. Andrew Nathan is chair of the advisory committee and Orville Schell is vice chair.

HUMAN RIGHTS WATCH

Human Rights Watch conducts regular, systematic investigations of human rights abuses in some seventy countries around the world. It addresses the human rights practices of governments of all political stripes, of all geopolitical alignments, and of all ethnic and religious persuasions. In internal wars it documents violations by both governments and rebel groups. Human Rights Watch defends freedom of thought and expression, due process and equal protection of the law; it documents and denounces murders, disappearances, torture, arbitrary imprisonment, exile, censorship and other abuses of internationally recognized human rights.

Human Rights Watch began in 1978 with the founding of its Helsinki division. Today, it includes five divisions covering Africa, the Americas, Asia, the Middle East, as well as the signatories of the Helsinki accords. It also includes five collaborative projects on arms transfers, children's rights, free expression, prison conditions, and women's rights. It maintains offices in New York, Washington, Los Angeles, London, Brussels, Moscow, Dushanbe, Rio de Janeiro, and Hong Kong. Human Rights Watch is an independent, nongovernmental organization, supported by contributions from private individuals and foundations worldwide. It accepts no government funds, directly or indirectly.

The staff includes Kenneth Roth, executive director; Cynthia Brown, program director; Holly J. Burkhalter, advocacy director; Ann S. Johnson, development director; Robert Kimzey, publications director; Jeri Laber, special advisor; Gara LaMarche, associate director; Lotte Leicht, Brussels Office Director; Juan Méndez, general counsel; Susan Osnos, communications director; Jemera Rone, counsel; Joanna Weschler, United Nations representative; and Derrick Wong, finance and administration director.

The regional directors of Human Rights Watch are Abdullahi An-Na'im, Africa; José Miguel Vivanco, Americas; Sidney Jones, Asia; Holly Cartner (acting), Helsinki; and Christopher E. George, Middle East. The project directors are Joost R. Hiltermann, Arms Project; Lois Whitman, Children's Rights Project; Gara LaMarche, Free Expression Project; and Dorothy Q. Thomas, Women's Rights Project.

The members of the board of directors are Robert L. Bernstein, chair; Adrian W. DeWind, vice chair; Roland Algrant, Lisa Anderson, Peter D. Bell, Alice L. Brown, William Carmichael, Dorothy Cullman, Irene Diamond, Edith Everett, Jonathan Fanton, Alan R. Finberg, Jack Greenberg, Alice H. Henkin, Harold Hongju Koh, Jeh Johnson, Stephen L. Kass, Marina Pinto Kaufman, Alexander MacGregor, Josh Mailman, Andrew Nathan, Jane Olson, Peter Osnos, Kathleen Peratis, Bruce Rabb, Orville Schell, Sid Sheinberg, Gary G. Sick, Malcolm Smith, Nahid Toubia, Maureen White, and Rosalind C. Whitehead.

Addresses for Human Rights Watch
485 Fifth Avenue, New York, NY 10017-6104
Tel: (212) 972-8400, Fax: (212) 972-0905, E-mail: hrwnyc@hrw.org

1522 K Street, N.W., #910, Washington, DC 20005-1202
Tel: (202) 371-6592, Fax: (202) 371-0124, E-mail: hrwdc@hrw.org

10951 West Pico Blvd., #203, Los Angeles, CA 90064-2126
Tel: (310) 475-3070, Fax: (310) 475-5613, E-mail: hrwatchla@igc.apc.org

33 Islington High Street, N1 9LH London, UK
Tel: (171) 713-1995, Fax: (171) 713-1800, E-mail: hrwatchuk@gn.apc.org

15 Rue Van Campenhout, 1040 Brussels, Belgium
Tel: (2) 732-2009, Fax: (2) 732-0471, E-mail: hrwatcheu@gn.apc.org

Gopher Address: gopher.humanrights.org port 5000

ACKNOWLEDGMENTS

Research for this report was undertaken in Nepal by Jeannine Guthrie, research associate for Human Rights Watch/Asia and in India by a research consultant who must remain anonymous. It was written by these researchers and edited by Sidney Jones, executive director of Human Rights Watch/Asia and by Jeri Laber, senior advisor to Human Rights Watch/Asia, with additional editorial advice from Sarah Lai of the Women's Rights Project, Andreas Stein of Human Rights Watch, and Juan Mendez, Human Rights Watch General Counsel. Jennifer Hyman, associate with Human Rights Watch/Asia prepared the manuscript for publication.

We wish to express our gratitude to the many organizations and individuals in Nepal and India who helped make this report possible, many of whom must remain anonymous. Special thanks are due the staff and members of the Informal Sector Service Centre (INSEC), Child Workers in Nepal (CWIN), INHURED International, ABC Nepal, the Creative Development Centre, and Women Acting Together for Change (WATCH), and to Meena Sharma, Shisam Mishra, and Shiva Hari Dahal for their invaluable assistance and advice during our visit to Nepal. We would also like to express our sincere thanks and admiration to S.A. Lalitha, of the Joint Women's Programme of India; Preeti Pai Patkar of *Prerana*, Anju Pawar, Farida Lambay, and the staff of Indian Health Organization for their aid and guidance to our researcher in India.

CONTENTS

I. INTRODUCTION

At least hundreds of thousands, and probably more than a million women and children are employed in Indian brothels. Many are victims of the increasingly widespread practice of trafficking in persons across international borders. In India, a large percentage of the victims are women and girls from Nepal. This report focuses on the trafficking of girls and women from Nepal to brothels in Bombay, where nongovernmental organizations say they comprise up to half of the city's estimated 100,000 brothel workers. Twenty percent of Bombay's brothel population is thought to be girls under the age of eighteen, and half of that population may be infected with the human immunodeficiency virus (HIV).[1]

Trafficking victims in India are subjected to conditions tantamount to slavery and to serious physical abuse. Held in debt bondage for years at a time, they are raped and subjected to other forms of torture, to severe beatings, exposure to AIDS, and arbitrary imprisonment. Many are young women from remote hill villages and poor border communities of Nepal who are lured from their villages by local recruiters, relatives or neighbors promising jobs or marriage, and sold for amounts as small as Nepali Rs.200 [$4.00] to brokers who deliver them to brothel owners in India for anywhere from Rs.15,000 to Rs.40,000 [$500-$1,333]. This purchase price, plus interest (reported to be ten percent of the total), becomes the "debt" that the women must work to pay off -- a process that can stretch on indefinitely. Only the brothel owner knows the terms of the debt, and most women have no idea how much they owe or the terms for repayment. Brothels are tightly controlled, and the girls are under constant surveillance. Escape is virtually impossible. Owners use threats and severe beatings to keep inmates in line. In addition, women fear capture by other brothel agents and arrest by the police if

---

[1]According to press reports, the Indian government's Human Resource Development Ministry released a report in May 1994, based on a survey conducted in 1991-1992 in six Indian cities. The study found 70,000-100,000 sex workers, of whom fifteen percent were under fifteen years of age when they entered prostitution; twenty-five percent were between sixteen and eighteen years. The study found that nearly twelve percent reported being tricked into entering the industry, and that fifty percent of all earnings went to brothel owners, pimps, police and local crime bosses. Most women surveyed reported being indebted for sums ranging from Rs. 10,000 to Rs. 15,000. (*Prostitution in Metropolitan Cities of India,* Central Social Welfare Board, Submitted to the Human Resource Development Ministry in August 1993, released May 1994, cited in *The Pioneer* (Delhi, India), June 15, 1994; *The Statesman* (Delhi, India), June 8, 1994; *Sunday Observer* (Delhi, India), October 3, 1993).

they are found on the streets; some of these police are the brothel owner's best clients. Many of the girls and women are brought to India as virgins; many return to Nepal with the HIV virus.

Both the Indian and Nepali governments are complicit in the abuses suffered by trafficking victims. These abuses are not only violations of internationally recognized human rights but are specifically prohibited under the domestic laws of both countries. The willingness of Indian and Nepali government officials to tolerate, and, in some cases, participate in the burgeoning flesh trade exacerbates abuse. Although human rights organizations in Nepal have reported extensively on the forced trafficking of Nepali girls to Indian brothels, and sensationalist coverage of trafficking issues is a regular feature of the local press, the great majority of cases is never publicized, and even when traffickers have been identified, there have been few arrests and fewer prosecutions.

In India, police and local officials patronize brothels and protect brothel owners and traffickers. Brothel owners pay protection money and bribes to the police to prevent raids and to bail out under-age girls who are arrested. Police who frequent brothels as clients sometimes seek out under-age girls and return later to arrest them -- a way of extorting bigger bribes. Girls and women who complain to the police about rape or abduction, or those who are arrested in raids or for vagrancy, are held in "protective custody" -- a form of detention. Corrupt authorities reportedly allow brothel owners to buy back detainees.

In Nepal, border police are also bribed to allow traffickers to transport girls to India. In many districts, traffickers exploit political connections to avoid arrest and prosecution. On return to Nepal, the few women who escape the brothels and appeal to the police for help, or who are returned by the Indian police, are shuttled from one police station to another as they make their way back to their home districts. Some remain in police detention for weeks until their guardians come and collect them. Women who have managed to survive the system of debt bondage frequently become recruiters to fulfill their owners' requirement that they find another girl to take their place. If women who return home have managed to earn money, they are more easily accepted back into their communities, and may eventually marry.[2] Those who escape the brothels before they have paid off their debts, who return without money, or who are sick and cannot work, are shunned by their families and communities. Many will return to India.

---

[2]However, the marriages rarely last longer than the money, and diseases contracted in the brothels often leave them sterile.

Existing laws in both countries have had virtually no effect on curbing trafficking.[3] Poor training, corruption and the lack of political will among senior government officials on both sides of the border means that the laws go unenforced. Officials also try to evade responsibility for the problem by categorizing trafficking as purely a social problem. Lack of transborder cooperation between India and Nepal compounds the problem. Apathy on the part of both governments, the highly organized nature of trafficking networks, police corruption and the patronage of influential government officials means virtual impunity for traffickers.

This report is based on interviews conducted with trafficking victims, most of them Nepali women in their twenties who were trafficked to India as teenagers or older women in Bombay who were still involved in the industry. The interviews are supplemented with case material and interview transcripts provided by social workers, human rights activists and representatives of other nongovernmental organizations who work on trafficking and AIDS-related issues, and interviews with government officials and police officers in Nepal and India between March and September 1994.

In Nepal, researchers visited the capital city of Kathmandu, villages in Nuwakot district and in the Pokhara valley, and the border towns of Birganj, Butwal and Bhairahawa. Human Rights Watch/Asia conducted interviews with police officers, activists and with seven women who had returned from India, all but one of whom stated that they had been forcibly trafficked for the purposes of prostitution. Methods of coercion ranged from false job or marriage offers to drugging and kidnapping. Four of these women were alleged to be HIV positive by neighbors or aid workers. Of the interviews, four are detailed accounts by women who had returned to Nepal within the last year. These four testified to the methods of force and coercion used by traffickers and provided information about areas of origin of victims and routes travelled, conditions in the brothels, the role of the Indian police, methods of escape and return, and treatment upon return, both by the authorities and by relatives.

In India, Human Rights Watch/Asia interviewed Nepali women still working in brothels, brothel owners, local doctors, activists, and lawyers in both Bombay and Delhi. We found that the nature of the business of forced prostitution directly affects research. The red-light districts in Bombay are the locus of a wide range of organized criminality, including smuggling, drugs, extortion, and trafficking. The network of underworld activities with their hierarchies of "dons"

---

[3] Indian anti-trafficking laws are designed to combat commercialized vice; prostitution, as such, is not illegal.

and their agents pervades the business of forced prostitution. In the brothels, fear of madams and pimps makes women reluctant to talk substantively with outsiders for any length of time. It is extremely difficult for researchers to speak to women alone, without the presence of a senior member of the brothel. Local activists who have spent years building up trust told Human Rights Watch/Asia that the information they receive appears to be amended as time passes and greater levels of trust are attained. We found many women were wary of requests for personal information. Ages were routinely masked by girls who were under the legal age of consent for sexual activity. Women who had escaped the industry reported having been coached by brothel owners to give set responses to questions about their ages, homes, villages and queries about how they ended up in prostitution. In addition to fear of retaliation from brothel management, a sense of shame and the sense that they lack any alternative to prostitution may also lead women to give misleading information about their route to this life.

While Nepalis are trafficked into many Indian cities, Human Rights Watch/Asia chose to focus on Bombay because it appears to have the highest concentration of Nepali girls and women in prostitution. In Bombay, according to the calculations of an organization of Nepali brothel staff,[4] there are about 20,000 Nepalis in the city's flesh trade -- other agencies estimate that the actual number is closer to 50,000. Most of these women and girls work for Nepali *gharwalis* (madams), and almost all are illiterate. Seventy percent are thought to belong to ethnic minority groups such as the Tamang, Gurung, Magar, and Sherpa. Women and girls from Nepal's Hindu majority communities comprise about ten to fifteen percent. Sixty percent of these girls and women are thought to have contracted HIV.[5]

In both Nepal and India, women who were or had been sex workers were hesitant to speak with researchers and reluctant to discuss their experiences except in the most general of terms, fearing reprisals from pimps, police and brothel owners, and the social stigma surrounding prostitution. Although most women with whom we spoke had some idea that forcible trafficking was illegal, and some had even attempted to make complaints against their traffickers after they returned to Nepal, few knew much about the legal process, or had been kept informed about the progress of their cases. Women who are trafficked into forced prostitution

---

[4]*Sanyukta Nepali Satya Shodhak Pidit Mahila Sangh* (United Nepali Organization for the Relief of Suffering Women).

[5]Indian Health Organization, "Tulasa and the Horrors of Child Prostitution," (IHO: Bombay, July 1993).

quickly learn to see police as their enemies, and to accept society's judgment that they themselves are criminals because they have engaged in prostitution, even if they have been beaten and raped into compliance.

While there has been some acknowledgement by government officials in both countries about the magnitude of the problem and the need for action, neither India nor Nepal has taken serious measures to stop trafficking. Despite a plethora of national and international legal instruments that address trafficking and abuses common in the industry, the trade continues to prosper. The burden of responsibility rests with India to stem the demand for new victims, and to protect the women and girls whose rights are violated on its territory. It must investigate and prosecute all those involved in trafficking and brothel operations, including police and other government agents who profit from the abuse. Nepal and India together should cooperate in police training for border operations. All reports of border police involvement in trafficking should be investigated and those responsible punished.

The international community also has a responsibility to see that both India and Nepal uphold their international obligations to prevent trafficking. Unfortunately, few governments have recognized this as a government responsibility, preferring to view the flesh trade as an unfortunate social evil with its roots in poverty. Trafficking in women and children has become an enormously profitable industry -- one that will not be stopped without international scrutiny and pressure.

II. POLITICAL AND ECONOMIC BACKGROUND

Nepal's extreme poverty and its economic and political relationship with India have facilitated the trafficking of Nepali women and girls to brothels in India. Nepal is a small, landlocked country that shares borders with two powerful nations -- China and India -- and depends on them for development assistance and trade; it also borders the tiny kingdom of Bhutan, approximately one sixth of whose population of some 600,000 currently reside as refugees in eastern Nepal.[1] Nepal is mountainous, with little infrastructure or industry. Ninety percent of its population of some nineteen million people reside in rural areas, dependent on subsistence agriculture.[2]

Nepal's large ethnic variety reflects its geography and includes people from the subtropical lowlands of the Terai on the Indian border, who have much in common with the people of northern India. The central hill dwellers share a mixture of Indian and Tibeto-Burman roots, and mountain people trace their origins to Central Asia and Tibet. For decades, members of these largely Buddhist communities like the Tamangs (the preponderant majority), Sherpas, Lamas and Gurungs have been targeted by brokers who supply women and girls to Indian brothels, children of both sexes for work in carpet and garment factories in Nepal and India, and people of all ages for road building and construction. The Tamangs live in large numbers in the remote hill villages of Nuwakot, Sindhupalchowk, Kavre and Dhading districts, but the search for jobs has scattered them in small numbers throughout the country.

Trafficking of women from Nepal's hill communities began in the nineteenth century, when the feudal Rana family, a line of prime ministers who ruled Nepal from 1846 to 1951, began recruiting Tamang girls from the Helambu (Yolmo) region of Sindhupalchowk, northeast of Kathmandu, to serve as

---

[1]NGOs are now investigating reports that Bhutanese girls and women are beginning to disappear out of the camps on Nepal's southeastern border. They fear these girls may have fallen victim to traffickers.

[2]Almost half of all Nepalese live below poverty level, meaning they receive less than 2,250 calories per day. Female literacy is estimated at twenty percent.(*Rights of the Child, Sale of children, child prostitution and child pornography, Report submitted by Mr. Vitit Muntarbhorn, Special Rapporteur, in accordance with Commission of Human Rights resolution 1993.82, Addendum, Visit by the Special Rapporteur to Nepal*, 20 January 1994, E/CN.4/1994/84/Add.1, p.3.) According to a 1990-91 World Bank Report, seventy percent of Nepal's population falls below the poverty line.

concubines for the ruler and his family. Owning concubines, or "Helambu girls," became a mark of high social status. The oligarchical Rana regime was overthrown by the hereditary monarchy in 1951, but the recruitment of women and girls continued, only now they were sold to brothel owners in India's red-light districts. The internationalization of trafficking in girls and women was due in part to a political alliance forged between Nepal and India in the last days of the Rana regime that opened the border between the two countries for travel and trade. Nuwakot, Sindhupalchok and other hill districts in the Bagmati Zone around Kathmandu became particularly notorious for trafficking. But as Indian demand for Nepali prostitutes grew, and the threat of AIDS increased the demand for new girls, girls from many castes[3] and communities and from other regions of Nepal were recruited for sale in Indian brothels. Today, instances of forced trafficking of women and girls for prostitution in India have been reported in virtually every district of Nepal and from all castes and ethnic groups.

POLITICAL STRUCTURE

Despite Nepal's transition to multi-party democracy in 1990, its towns and villages remain tightly controlled by powerful local leaders, many of them members of wealthy families who have traditionally dominated village life. Under the previous single-party system, termed *"panchayat* democracy," these local bosses gained political influence beyond their home districts, nurturing the growth of a complex network of political patronage.

The panchayat system, which was established by King Mahendra in 1962, was a four-tiered system which provided for popular elections only at the local level, where the electorate was easily controlled by local landowners.[4] The 1962

---

[3]The caste system in Nepal, as in India, is a system of social stratification derived from Hindu concepts of ritual purity and pollution. Caste status is inherited. Among traditional Hindus, intermarriage, the sharing of food and other contact between members of different castes is prohibited.

[4]Two years earlier, King Mahendra had dissolved the parliament and cabinet, banned political parties, and instituted direct rule. Under the 1962 Constitution and *"panchayat democracy,"* each village or group of villages with a population of 2,000 or more elected an eleven-member village panchayat. The members of these local panchayats elected the seventy-five district panchayats, whose members elected the fourteen zonal panchayats. Members of the latter then elected the *Rastriya* (national) Panchayat. The king ruled as absolute monarch, advised by a Council of Ministers and the Palace Secretariat.

Constitution also provided for a prime minister, nominated by the king, and prohibited political parties. Nepal was declared an "independent, indivisible, and sovereign Hindu state" with the king as the ultimate source of executive, legislative and judicial powers.[5]

From the start, the power of the panchayat was land and caste-based and plagued by local rivalries and factionalism. Poor and landless villagers were compelled by necessity to choose sides, allying themselves with a patron who could provide them with work. This created an ideal environment for the development of trafficking networks and criminal gangs. According to one scholar:

> Once in power, group leaders...traditionally used political positions to strengthen private networks by dispensing patronage, in addition to enriching themselves.

> These patron-client hierarchies were also reflected in the ties between *Rastriya* [National] *Panchayat* ... members and their local factions. The absence of political parties exacerbated the formation of personality-based coalitions among members of the *Rastriya Panchayat*. These nation-level factions were generally geographically oriented, centered on assembly members with large government-run facilities or projects in their districts. At every level, politics under the Partyless *Panchayat* System was characterized by intra-elite struggles for control of government resources.[6]

In 1972 King Mahendra was succeeded by his son, King Birendra. The panchayat system, altered in 1980 to provide for the direct election of the *Rastriya Panchayat* based on universal adult suffrage, remained in force until April 1990, when a massive pro-democracy movement led to the adoption of a multi-party system. Since then, other political forces have begun to make inroads into local administration. The government of Prime Minister Girija Prasad Koirala, of the Nepali Congress Party, was elected by popular vote in May 1991. On July 10, 1994, Koirala resigned after his government lost an important parliamentary vote.

---

[5]Although Hinduism is the dominant religion in Nepal, there are significant numbers of Buddhists, animists, Christians and Muslims.

[6]Jeffrey Riedinger,"Prospects for Land Reform in Nepal," *South Asia Bulletin*, Vol.XIII, Nos 1&2 (New York: South Asia Bulletin, 1993), p.24.

Elections were held November 13, 1994, two years ahead of schedule, and a Communist government under Manmohan Adhikary took power.

But former panchayat members still wield substantial power locally and allegations of corruption and political patronage of criminal gangs -- traffickers of human beings, drugs, and precious metals in particular -- persist and are apparently well-founded. Politicians who have gained power through the electoral process are also now accused of engaging in similar activities.[7]

Under the 1990 constitution, the king retains executive power, and appoints the leader of the parliamentary party commanding an elected majority in the House of Representatives as his prime minister. The political relationship between royalists (largely former panchayat members), who still wield significant power at the local level, and the elected leadership remains uneasy. The government appears to have insufficient control over the police force, the principal violator of human rights in Nepal.

ECONOMIC FACTORS

The flourishing trade in Nepali women and girls in India must be understood in the context of economic conditions in both countries. Nepal's extreme poverty makes recruiting in its rural villages easy and profitable. Because of its economic dependence on India and the political ties between the powerful Nepali Congress Party and the Indian government[8] the previous government of Nepal was inhibited from regulating the border or actively combating cross-border crime unless the Indian government also committed itself to stemming demand by enforcing anti-trafficking laws.

In the past decade Nepal has undergone increased industrialization in urban areas such as Kathmandu and in towns in the Terai, the lowland area along Nepal's southern border with India. This growth was made possible by trade agreements between India and Nepal and reflects much Indian investment. Many new businesses in Nepal are Indian-owned or employ Indian workers. Indian

---

[7]Human rights organizations in Nepal report that since Adhikary took office, there has been an apparent increase in the number of trafficking-related arrests, judging from reports in the local press. Activists express hope that this indicates a new willingness on the part of the Nepal's government to prosecute some offenders.

[8]India provided significant support to Nepal's democracy movement in 1990 and had long provided a haven for members of the exiled opposition Nepali Congress Party.

industries south of the border recruit large numbers of Nepali workers who bring currency back into Nepal.[9] Import of Indian products and export of Nepali resources, including timber, is growing rapidly.

Despite this growth in urban areas, there has been little change in Nepal's rural economy, which remains largely dependent on subsistence agriculture. Many rural villages are very far from urban markets where crops could be sold if a surplus existed. In most cases there is little surplus and hill villages suffer lean periods at the end of each growing season -- hence the attraction of work in the city. In addition, despite government efforts at land reform, most tillable land in rural Nepal is owned by a few influential, often high caste families. Members of lower castes and poorer ethnic groups have difficulty sustaining themselves on their meager landholdings and are engaged in a continuous search for new ways to generate income.

Tamang peasants are among Nepal's most impoverished minority groups. Today, according to Jyothi Sanghera, an activist who presented her findings to the U.N. Working Group on Contemporary Forms of Slavery in 1991, an average Tamang family owns less than one hectare of unirrigated land. Most were already tenants before Nepal implemented a series of land reform acts in the 1950s, at which time the vast majority were evicted -- left landless or with small plots of arid land on steep hill slopes. No longer able to survive on subsistence farming, and with virtually no access to education or other means of entry into a cash-based economy, the Tamang were forced to migrate in search of other means of support. They found it in low-paying seasonal work as porters or manual laborers in the lowlands, or on road construction sites in India. Tamang men were also recruited for the Gurkha regiments of the British and Indian armies. But these communities soon found there was another, more lucrative way to earn money. "A commodity... has been created that sells, and sell[s] very well at that, in the labour market of the sex industry: the body and sexual labour of the Tamang woman..."[10]

---

[9] India's economy also benefits from a steady supply of cheap Nepali labor, particularly in its textile and carpet factories along the border. Many workers attracted to these industries are children. A Nepali border patrol officer told Human Rights Watch/Asia that thousands of people crossed the border at his post each day, and many said they were seeking work in a carpet factory that had recently opened in nearby Gorakpur, India. Most were nine or ten-year-old boys.

[10] Jyoti Sanghera, Federation Internationale Terre des Hommes, "Prevention of Traffic in Persons and the exploitation of the prostitution of others; Trafficking and sexploitation of Nepali girl children and women in the sex industry," Presentation at the session of the

Border towns on both sides are bustling markets, catering to residents from both countries seeking jobs and bargains. They also provide a natural market for smuggling and prostitution, serving as a nexus for brokers and agents who take advantage of the crowds of anonymous travellers, the guest lodges, and the easy access to transportation.

A 1950 treaty with Nepal provided for free passage and trade across the Nepal/India border.[11] Article 7 of the treaty reads:

> The Government of India and Nepal agree to grant, on a reciprocal basis, to the nationals of one country in the territories of the other the same privileges in the matters of residence, ownership of property, participation in trade and commerce, movement and other privileges of a similar nature.[12]

Successive governments of Nepal expressed dissatisfaction with the treaty several times, but although either country could terminate the treaty with a year's notice, India has not wished to lose the privileges it enjoys, and Nepal cannot

---

U.N. Working group on Contemporary Forms of Slavery, Geneva, July 29 to August 2, 1991. Note: The practice of leaving Nepal's hill villages in search of work abroad is referred to in Nepal as "*lahur*" and is a well-established tradition in Nuwakot and Sindhupalchowk districts. *Lahures*, or economic migrants, provide many villages with their only source of cash income. The tradition probably began with the recruitment of Nepal's indigenous minorities into the Gurkha regiments, but now refers to all work abroad, including prostitution.

[11]Contemporary relations between India and Nepal developed out of post-World War II India's concern about the possible spread of communism. In 1949 China declared its intent to "liberate" Tibet and re-establish China's "traditional" boundaries in the frontier region. Newly independent India recognized China's claim to Tibet, but sought to limit Chinese communist influence on Nepal and the neighboring Himalayan kingdoms of Bhutan and Sikkim by strengthening the "Himalayan frontier policy" introduced by the British and signing treaties of peace and cooperation with the three kingdoms. The 1950 treaty was signed by the Rana regime soon before it was overthrown and included a mutual security agreement.

[12]United Nations Treaty Series 3, "India-Nepal Security Relations and the 1950 Treaty; Time for New Perspectives," *Asian Survey,* Vol. XXXIV, No. 3, March 1994. pp.274-5.

afford the consequences of a deterioration in its trade relationship with India.[13] On February 9, 1995, India announced that it was ready to hold talks with Nepal's new government on amending the forty-five-year-old treaty.

The effect of the open border policy on the prevention of trafficking of women is clear. No passports, visas or residence permits are required for nationals traveling between India and Nepal. Because people pass freely between the two countries for work, shopping and business (according to Nepali police, up to 100,000 people per day through one popular border post), it is extremely difficult for border police to check illegal activity. Traffickers and their victims move easily across the border, and the onus is on individual police officers to stop and question suspicious-looking travellers. The problem is compounded by consistent reports of police corruption on both sides of the border.

In India's red-light districts, the demand for Nepali girls, especially virgins with fair skin and Mongolian features, continues to increase. It is impossible to say how many girls and women are employed in the sex industry in India or what percentage of the total is from Nepal. Estimates have been based largely on the numbers of women employed by brothels in urban areas, but prostitution exists in every city and town in India and in many villages, and statistics vary enormously. Dr. I.S. Gilada, general secretary of the Indian Health Organization (IHO), estimated in various studies conducted between 1985 and 1994 that there were between 70,000 and 100,000 prostitutes in Bombay, 100,000 in Calcutta, 40,000 in Delhi, 40,000 in Pune and 13,000 in Nagpur. Based on his statistics, Nepali social workers estimate the number of Nepali girls and women now working in Indian brothels at about 200,000 and believe that between 5,000 and 7,000 new Nepalis end up in Indian brothels every year. The Indian Council of Medical

---

[13]In March 1989, angered by Nepal's import of Chinese arms (instead of arms manufactured in India) and its requirement that Indian workers in Nepal apply for work permits, India closed all but two of the twenty-one bilateral trade routes between India and Nepal and thirteen of fifteen transit routes through India used by Nepal for international trade. The move was economically devastating for Nepal and probably hastened the fall of the old regime. India restored the former trade relationship a little over a year later by signing a joint communiqué with the new prime minister in June 1990, in which Nepal agreed it would not buy weapons from China without consulting India, rescinded the work permit requirement for Indians, and granted them other concessions. Nepal's need to maintain its relationship with India, whatever the cost, and India's power to disrupt Nepal's economy was lost on no one.

Research estimates the total number of prostitutes in India at about one million.[14] By contrast, the Bharatiya Patita Udhar Sabha (Indian Association for the Rescue of Fallen Women), a voluntary organization dedicated to the welfare of the country's sex workers, estimates that in 1992 there were more than 8 million brothel workers in India and another 7.5 million call girls.[15] There is simply no way to verify these statistics, but it is clear the percentage of Nepali girls in Indian brothels is very high, that their numbers appear to be increasing, and that the average age at which they are recruited is significantly lower than it was ten years ago, dropping from fourteen to sixteen years in the 1980s to ten to fourteen years in 1994. Dr. Gilada of IHO told our researcher that the youngest girl he had seen in a Bombay brothel was nine years old.

While Human Rights Watch/Asia has chosen to focus on Bombay because it is the city which appears to have the highest percentage of Nepali prostitutes, Nepali women are trafficked into many other Indian cities. Of the roughly 3,500 women in prostitution in Delhi's red-light district of G.B. Road, activists estimate that about 150 are from Nepal.[16] In Calcutta, various studies conducted by the All India Institute of Hygiene and Public Health (AIIHPH) in 1993 estimate that 20 percent of the 5,000 sex workers in the Sonagachi red-light area are Nepali. According to one AIIHPH expert, over 500 Nepali girls arrived in Sonagachi in 1993 alone.[17] In the state of Gujarat, which borders Maharashtra, a survey undertaken by the International Society for Research on Civilisation Diseases and Environment estimates that of the total number of persons in prostitution in Surat

---

[14]*The Telegraph* (Calcutta, India), "Green Signal for the Red Light," February 22, 1994.

[15] *The Telegraph* (Calcutta, India), January 5, 1992. Note: "Sex workers" or "commercial sex workers" refers to all people engaged in prostitution. The term is favored by many activists working for the rights of persons in the commercial sex industry. However, many activists in India who work with trafficking victims object to its use when referring to their clients, because they prefer to focus on the involuntary nature of trafficking. "Street prostitutes" refer to persons who solicit customers in public places, "call girls" generally operate from homes, flats or hotel rooms and serve customers by appointment.

[16]Interview with SA.Lalitha, Community Organizer, Joint Women's Program, New Delhi, India, July 1994.

[17]*The Telegraph*, "Nepal Girl-runners Turn to City," (Calcutta, India) December 1, 1993.

city, 80 percent were from outside the state, with 10 percent of these persons from Nepal. The voluntary organization also found that many persons in prostitution in Bombay periodically visited Surat because of the market for prostitution there.[18]

Although tourism is an important industry in both countries, and sex tourism appears to be on the increase in India, tourism is less a factor in the sex industry than local demand. All of the women Human Rights Watch/Asia interviewed reported that most of their customers were Indian. Some were also Nepali, although in at least one case Nepali customers were discouraged, for fear they would help Nepali girls escape.

Brothels are big business. Despite expenses incurred in employing a network of agents to recruit new workers in Nepal (some procurers are reportedly paid up to Indian Rs.6,000 [about $200] per trip) and protection money that is paid weekly to police and local crime bosses (said to total Rs.200 [$6.60] per brothel inmate per week), even the cheapest of brothels can turn a substantial profit, generally collecting from Rs.50-Rs.100 [$1.66-$3.33] per client, with much more for special services. A brothel may employ anywhere from four to fifty workers, and an inmate may serve more than fifteen clients a day, on an average of twenty-six to twenty-eight days a month. The brothel owners generally provide no more than two meals a day and most workers are allowed to keep only the tips from their clients, Rs 2 to 5 (fifteen cents or less) per man. With these meager resources, they must cover their own expenses for food, clothing, and personal effects. The cost of medical care is typically paid by the owner, and then added to a inmate's "debt" -- sometimes with interest. The owner, who frequently owns more than one brothel, clearly stands to make a profit, but agents, local police and others involved in the industry also benefit. As one former prostitute told Human Rights Watch/Asia, "Police, doctors, *dalals* (pimps), they are all fed by the brothels."

---

[18]*Times of India*, "Plan to Help Surat Sex Workers" (Bombay), August 8, 1994, p.5.

III. PATTERNS OF ABUSE

There are two distinct patterns to the trafficking of girls and women from Nepal. The best known and oldest involves the enticement of mainly Tamang girls from hill districts where the flesh trade has become an almost traditional source of income. But the incidence of forced trafficking from other parts of Nepal is also on the rise.[1] Poor migrant women and children whose families have moved to Nepal's urban areas in search of employment are the principal victims. These girls and women come from all castes and ethnic groups. Human Rights Watch/Asia visited Nepal and interviewed women from several areas of Nepal who had been trafficked to India and had returned. In all cases, families, neighbors and friends play an active role in forced trafficking by concocting fictitious marriage and job offers, contacting recruiters and brokers, or simply luring girls away from home on outings or errands, kidnapping and selling them. Regardless of the victims' origins, their reports of abuse in Indian brothels are remarkably consistent.

The average age of the thousands of Nepali girls recruited every year for prostitution in brothels in India has reportedly dropped in the past decade 0from fourteen to sixteen years in the 1980s, to ten to fourteen in 1991, despite new laws promulgated in both countries in 1986 designed to stem trafficking and child prostitution.[2] Police in areas with a high incidence of trafficking state that the average age of new trafficking victims is about thirteen. However, trafficking victims are frequently coached by captors to conceal their true ages. Girls forced into prostitution in Bombay's brothels may remain trapped in the brothel system for

---

[1]Trafficked Nepali women sometimes conceal their villages or towns of origin. For example, all the Nepalis in activist Preeti Pai Patkar's study said they came from one of three major areas: Chitwan, Narayanghat, or Nuwakot District. The activist noted that this was a suspiciously narrow range of answers. Not one girl said she came from a more remote region, despite evidence to the contrary. None reported coming from villages in Sindhupalchowk, where an enormous amount of trafficking occurs. There might be several reasons for this. While it is possible that these answers were an attempt at deliberate obfuscation, research by Human Rights Watch/Asia found that many *kothas*, or brothel compounds, are operated by and employ women from one specific area. Girls from Nuwakot and Sindhupalchowk work for madams from their own communities, madams from eastern Nepal recruit girls from eastern Nepal. It is possible that activists might have more contact with women from one region's kothas rather than from others.

[2] Sanghera, Federation Internationale Terre des Hommes, Presentation to the U.N. Working Group on Contemporary Forms of Slavery, Geneva, July 29 to August 2, 1991.

more than ten years, during which time they may be sold from one brothel to another many times.

CASE HISTORIES

The following cases, based on interviews conducted by Human Rights Watch/Asia in March 1994 with young women in Nepal who had returned from Bombay, and in July 1994 with women still employed in Bombay's brothels, describe some of the patterns typical of trafficking between Nepal and India. The first, "Maya" represents a case of simple abduction. Although she filed a complaint against her traffickers, no one was ever prosecuted.

"Maya"

"Maya" is from a small village in Nuwakot district. She is twenty-three, but looks much older. She has dark circles under her eyes; her skin is dry and lined. A local health worker thinks she was ejected from a brothel in Bombay after testing positive for HIV, a story Maya denies. Maya said she first left her village when she was eighteen and returned to her village in July 1993, after spending three years in an Indian brothel.

Maya was married to a man from a nearby village when she was around thirteen. Soon after, her husband began seeing someone else. He moved out when Maya was sixteen, married a second wife and took her to Kathmandu. Maya had lived alone for two years when her father-in-law told her she should follow her husband to Kathmandu. He took her there. At her husband's house she was beaten and treated very badly.

In 1990 a fellow villager began visiting the house. The second time he came to visit, he brought another man along. They invited Maya and her husband to come out to see a movie. Maya's husband told her to go ahead without him. The three of them boarded a bus, which Maya said kept going farther and farther from Kathmandu. Eventually, they went through the border at Kakarbhitta. They were never stopped or questioned by the police.

After two days traveling by bus, they reached Bombay and the men left Maya at a house and told her they would pick her up the next day. They never came back. Maya realized she was in a brothel when she saw that the house was occupied by about twenty-five women, all but three of whom were from Nepal. Two or three were girls she had known from her own village. The brothel where Maya worked was called a "pillow house," lowest in the brothel hierarchy where most new girls start out. It was a large building, with several rooms where the women lived, slept and worked. There were eight beds in each room and curtains dividing the beds. All of the girls' and women's earnings were turned over to the brothel owner, a woman named Renu Tamang from Urleni in Nuwakot district. The women worked from noon to 1:00 A.M. They were given no days off. After a year, the owner told Maya that the broker had been paid for her and that she was responsible for paying back her purchase price, but she was never told how much she owed. The owner told her she could go home only after she paid off her debt. Maya noted that another brothel inmate, a woman from Trisuli, had worked there for thirteen years and had never managed to pay off her debt.

Maya was beaten severely for the first four or five days she was held in the brothel because she refused to have sex with customers. They continued to beat her until she submitted. Later on, she was beaten with bottles and thick sticks because she was not earning enough. She said that all the brothel inmates were beaten if they did not earn enough. Her customers included Indians and foreigners -- Germans, Singaporeans, Filipinos and Saudi Arabians. The customers would select the women they wanted, and the women could not refuse, or they would be beaten.

In the three years Maya was held in the brothel, she never received any form of contraception. Girls who became pregnant would be given abortions. The brothel did not provide condoms, but occasionally customers brought their own. Maya said that she never asked clients to use condoms because she did not know they could prevent AIDS. She said she had heard about AIDS, but did not know anything about it. Because she stayed in the brothel only a short time, she did not know the symptoms.

After one year in Bombay, Maya began to get sick. She developed a high fever and was taken to the doctor who gave her an injection, but she did not know what it was. She then returned to work. Maya told Human Rights Watch/Asia that she and two other girls, one from Sindhupalchok who was sick, and one from Gorkha, decided to escape from the brothel. All of them had been beaten often and thought they should flee to save their lives. Maya said that while some police officers often came as clients to the brothel, one branch of the police force frequently raided the brothel looking for child prostitutes. The three women appealed to these police to help them escape, and the police took them to the border and handed them over to the Hanuman Dhoka police station in Kathmandu. Maya was sent on to the police in Ranipowa and then Trisuli, where she was held in detention for ten days. From there it took her six days to reach Nuwakot. As Maya understood the police policy on returnees, the police inform the girl's family by letter and then hold her until relatives come to collect her.

Maya and the two other women filed complaints at the Hanuman Dhoka police station in Kathmandu, and the police told them that they would be informed once the traffickers were found, but as far as she knows, no one was ever arrested.

Maya's health deteriorated after her return. She lost weight and suffered from diarrhea, high fevers and stomach aches. Since returning to the village, her health has improved slightly. In January 1994, she was treated with traditional medicine and feels that she has been cured, although she remains very tired and weak and cannot work. Local health workers suspect Maya may not have escaped but was ejected from the brothel in India because she had contracted HIV.

"Tara"

At thirty-four or thirty-five years old, "Tara" is a senior woman in a brothel in Bombay. She was described as the "in-charge" of the younger brothel inmates by a local activist. Senior women like Tara are frequently used by gharwalis to keep track of newer inmates. They watch for escape attempts, listen for forbidden conversations with customers, and accompany younger girls when they leave the premises for medical treatment. The interview with Tara was instructive because it reflected both her experiences as a young trafficking victim, and her attitudes now which are closer to those of brothel management.

Tara arrived in Bombay eighteen or nineteen years ago when she was sixteen years old. She told Human Rights Watch/Asia that she grew up in Nuwakot jilla [district] and got trapped into prostitution when she went with two girlfriends to see the cigarette factories at Janakpur, on the Nepal/India border.

> We fell into the clutches of a dalali [procuress] -- a Nepali dalali at that. We were three girls together, in the beginning. We spent two years together, but then we were separated. I don't know what happened to the other two girls. I often wonder what happened to them. When I was captured, I could not escape or return to my home: they would have caught me for sure. If I had known what was to happen to me, I would have killed myself halfway. [But] leaving this life is not an option for me, I simply cannot think about it. My purity was violated, so I thought: why go back, go back to what? I may as well just stay here. If I ever catch that damn dalali, I don't know what I would do to her. If I ever catch her, you have simply no idea what I will do to her.

Tara described her bewilderment upon arrival in Bombay:

> When they brought me here, it was in a taxi. I kept looking
> around, wondering what kind of work was going on in this area
> of this big city. Everywhere I looked, I saw curtained doorways
> and rooms in this area. Men would go and come through these
> curtained entrances. People on the street would be calling out,
> "Two rupees, two rupees." I asked the other Nepali women if
> these were offices; it seemed the logical explanation. In two days
> I knew everything. I cried.

The building in Bombay where Tara lives and works has two floors, and probably houses about fifty women. There are two "maliks" [bosses] for the building. Tara said there were four rooms on her floor, and four Nepali girls and two Indian in her room. She said that when she first came, there were mostly Nepali girls working there, and a Nepali gharwali. Now both Indian and Nepalis work together. She said that like her, these younger Nepali girls came from the mountain areas of Nepal.

Despite the fact that Tara was herself an unwilling victim of the industry, she remained caught in the system for nearly twenty years and is now a senior inmate with management responsibilities. Her testimony, bitter when referring to the past or to women who have managed to escape, was generally sympathetic to her gharwali -- with whom she probably shares a similar history. The fact that she has not attempted to return to Nepal or to open her own establishment suggests that she has not escaped the cycle of debt.

> Many girls return to their home area, build houses. Money is
> everything. It gets you acceptance in the village. There is no one
> in Nepal who does not know about Bombay, and this business,
> not one person in Nepal. The gharwali is good to the girls and
> does not harm them. She makes the food arrangements, takes
> care of their needs. It is when a girl falls into the clutches of bad
> men, thugs, goondas [thugs], that she is defiled by them, and ill-
> treated in many ways.

Tara's testimony reflects some of the most persistent myths of the trafficking industry -- that all prostitution is voluntary and driven by economic hardship, and that many prostitutes become rich and return home. Brothel inmates report being coached to give stock answers to questions from investigators and curious customers, and oft-repeated success stories help keep inmates striving to earn. "Santhi," a woman whose case is described below, told Human Rights Watch/Asia "In the brothels we were told by the owner to tell the police we came by ourselves because we didn't have food. We were told to say we were twenty-five years old. If we didn't say that we would be beaten." A relief worker who had done research in Bombay and knows Santhi says brothel inmates she interviewed gave her similar answers when she questioned them about their past.

THE PATH TO BOMBAY

The Nepali girls and women who were interviewed by Human Rights Watch/Asia were forcibly trafficked into India. They did not work as prostitutes voluntarily but were held in conditions tantamount to slavery. Promises of jobs and marriage are common techniques by which recruiters entice their victims to leave home. But other, more overtly coercive tactics such as kidnapping are also reported. Girls who are already in debt bondage in other industries, particularly carpet factories, are particularly vulnerable.

The Traffickers

Traffickers are most typically men in their twenties or thirties or women in their thirties and forties who have travelled the route to the city several times and know the hotels to stay in and the brokers to contact. Traffickers frequently work in groups of two or more. Male and female traffickers are sometimes referred to as *dalals and dalalis*, (commission agents) who are either employed by a brothel owner directly, or operate more or less independently. Professional agents who recruit for the bigger brothels reportedly may be paid up to Rs.6,000 [$200] per girl. But most traffickers are small-time, local recruiters who earn considerably less. In either case, to stay in business they need the patronage of local bosses and the protection afforded by bribes to the police.

Female traffickers are referred to as *didi* or *phupu didi* (literally, paternal aunt). In Nuwakot district, according to local activists, the majority of *didis* are returned prostitutes from five or six Village Development Committees (VDCs) in eastern Nuwakot.[3] The peak trafficking months in Nuwakot and Sindhupalchowk are between June and late August or early September when the *didis* return to the villages to participate in local festivals and to recruit girls to bring back to the cities. These months precede the harvest, when poverty is felt most acutely, making it easy to recruit.

> People become especially vulnerable every year from June to August, which are known as the "hungry months." At this time, every mountain village of Nepal suffers from more than the usual level of poverty, while they wait for the new harvests. Villagers have depleted their store of grains, and their hunger drives them to the local moneylender and feudal lord. This impossible situation has forced many young people from the mountain villages to urban centres, where they search for employment and a better future. Most young men work in factories, transportation, and construction, whereas the young girls and women work in garment and carpet factories, and in domestic service. A proportion of the young women will disappear to India.[4]

Family members -- uncles, cousins, stepfathers -- also act as trafficking agents. Of seven trafficking victims interviewed by Human Rights Watch/Asia in March 1994, six were trafficked to India with the help of close family friends or relatives. In each case, the victim complained of deception.

---

[3]Nepal is divided into five development regions, fourteen zones and seventy-five districts. Under the panchayat system these zones were administered by "zonal panchayats," which fed into the Rastriya Panchayat, but since 1990, zones no longer function as administrative units. Districts are broken down into subsectors called "village development committees" (VDCs), and "municipalities." There are 3,995 VDCs in Nepal and thirty-six municipalities. VDCs are the smallest local administrative unit. The Villager Development Committees of Betini, Bal Kumari, Sikharbeshi, Gyanphedi, Samundratar and Gaunkharka are noted as centers for trafficking. Urleni VDC is also the alleged home village for several brothel owners.

[4]Gauri Pradan, "The Road to Bombay: Forgotten Women; Maya and Parvati: The End of a Dream," *Red Light Traffic, the Trade in Nepali Girls* (Nepal: ABC Nepal, 1992), p.33.

Girls are recruited in a number of ways. Village girls and their
families are often deceived by smartly dressed young men who
arrive in the village claiming to have come from Kathmandu and
offering marriage and all the comforts of modern urban life.
They go through a local ceremony and leave the village never to
be seen again. The girls end up in Indian brothels.

Sometimes older men promise the girls employment in the city.
Another avenue is through distant relatives or friends who
pretend to arrange a marriage with relatives or friends in another
village, but instead abduct the girl and send her to India.
Sometimes a trusted individual abducts the girl on the pretext of
educating her in India.[5]

Trafficking appears to be on the increase throughout Nepal and to be
growing most rapidly in areas where it has so far received the least attention --
towns and villages along the east-west highway, border towns, tourist centers and,
according to some reports, the camps that house Bhutanese refugees in Jhapa
district in eastern Nepal.[6]

Local women who have returned from India are also employed as
recruiters. These women are exceptionally well-placed to identify potential
trafficking victims because they already know the local girls and their families.

Women who are already in the sex trade and have graduated to the level
of brothel keepers, managers or even owners travel through the villages of their
own and neighboring districts in search of young girls. Though not very typical, the
following story encapsulates the essence of the dream of success and glamour that
these women symbolize to the simple village girls.

---

[5]Omar Sattur, Anti-Slavery International and Child Workers of Nepal Concerned
Centre, *Child Labor in Nepal,* No. 13 (Kathmandu: ASI's Child Labour Series, 1993),
p.60.

[6] Dr. Aruna Upreti of the Women's Rehabilitation Centre, a relief organization in
Calcutta, told a journalist with *The Telegraph* in December 1993 that the number of
Nepalis in Calcutta's brothels had doubled in the past year. She said that besides a large
number of Tamang girls from Nepal's hill districts, Bhutanese girls from the refugee
camps in eastern Nepal were arriving in India, and that girls from the southern town of
Butwal had been found in places as far away as Hong Kong. *The Telegraph,*"Nepal Girl-
runners Turn to City," (Calcutta, India) December 1, 1993.

Only a short time before my visit, a madam had alighted upon this remote hill village in Sindhupalchowk in a helicopter rented from Kathmandu, for which she must have had to pay a sum of about $1,000. She descended like a celestial fairy mother in the midst of these poor village folk, in all her resplendent finery, and doled out little gifts of baubles and cosmetics to the starry-eyed adolescent girls....When this madam left the village, seven young girls disappeared with her.[7]

The typical agent is far less glamorous, and the number of Nepali prostitutes who manage to become wealthy in India is minuscule. Most recruiters are women desperately trying to escape the abuse and debt bondage of the brothel system themselves.

Perhaps the most pernicious and lamentable examples in this category are those women who are themselves forced into prostitution and who have been told by their brothelkeepers that the only way they can procure their release is by furnishing a substitute. At any given time, several of these women travel to their villages in the hope of cajoling a younger female relative, a friend or just another village woman to accompany them. Most often they are successful...and return with another victim, in lieu of themselves. However, once free they do not make an exit from the prostitution market, they merely end up working as... [independent] prostitutes and finally hope to set up their own little shop with five women working under them...[8]

These local agents buy girls from their families, sometimes for as little as Nepali Rs.200 [$4], or tempt them with promises of future earnings, and take them to the Indian border where they are sold to a broker or for anything from Indian

---

[7]Sanghera, Federation Internationale Terre des Hommes. This story is frequently repeated in Nepal to illustrate the enormous wealth accumulated by some Bombay brothel owners. Some newspaper reports identify the madam as Simla Tamang, who was convicted of trafficking in 1993 . According to press reports, Simla Tamang admitted in court to owning brothels in Bombay which employed some five hundred prostitutes. The Simla Tamang case is discussed at length below .

[8]Sanghera, p.7.

Rs.1,000-Rs.8,000 [$22-$266]. These middlemen then sell them to brothel owners in Bombay and elsewhere for Rs.15,000-Rs.50,000 [$500 - $1,666], depending on the girl's age and beauty. Virgins command higher prices.

"Padma"

"Padma" is the *gharwali* of a small brothel in Bombay. She told Human Rights Watch/Asia that like many others, she came to India as a young girl, from a remote village in the mountains of Nepal. After twenty years in the profession she now runs a brothel which employs between three and six girls.

> It took us six days of trekking to get to Kathmandu. Nowadays there is a bus service, so it is not so bad. Can you imagine: Six days! That was really bad. I don't know anyone else in the profession from my own village, but I know others, a couple of others, from neighboring villages. In my house ['ghar'], there are usually three or four girls. Sometimes there are six, but that is the maximum. There is no fixed number. In fact, there really is no telling from moment to moment. Just last month, two new girls arrived.

Carpet Factories

Carpets are Nepal's most important export and, along with tourism, one of its most essential industries. Besides being notorious in their own right for appalling working conditions, the pervasive use of child labor and debt bondage,[9] Kathmandu carpet factories have been important recruitment centers for Indian brothels. In 1994 it was estimated that half of all Nepal's carpet workers are

---

[9]US Department of Labor, *By the Sweat and Toil of Children; the Use of Child Labor in American Imports, A Report to the Committee on Appropriation, United States Congress, July 15, 1994*, pp. 119-122. Note: Between July and November 1994, Nepal's export of carpets dropped by 36 percent when sales to Germany, Nepal's largest importer, slowed after a television broadcast aroused public concern over Nepal's use of child labor. CWIN reported in January 1995 that the use of child labor in the organized sector began to decrease as a result of international pressure.

children. Girls and boys from poor rural hill families, 47 percent of them Tamang,[10] are recruited from their villages and sold or apprenticed to factory owners. Brokers working within the carpet factories select likely girls and entice them into leaving the factory with offers of better jobs elsewhere -- a relatively easy task since many carpet workers are themselves caught in a state of debt bondage where they receive no wages. The brokers then arrange for their transport to India, frequently with the complicity of friends and family members.

Child Workers in Nepal Concerned Centre (CWIN), a Kathmandu-based organization dedicated to the rights of children, reported in 1994 that of 300 Nepali prostitutes interviewed in Bombay, 40 percent had been trafficked from carpet factories.[11] In March 1994, A.R. Panday, the chief district officer of Nuwakot confirmed that the trafficking network that operates in Nuwakot district used the carpet industry in Kathmandu as a secondary point of recruitment.

> Guardians will send girls to Kathmandu as laborers. There they learn a more sophisticated life, and then will be tempted by a broker who takes them up to the border. The carpet industry employs backward castes -- Danuwar, Himal, Tamang.... Girls are attracted by idea of work in the city, they are ambitious. The broker works from inside the factory, selects a girl and convinces her to go with him and then takes her to the border and sells her.[12]

Sexual abuse of girls in carpet factories is commonplace. Almost half of the more than twelve hundred girls under sixteen working in carpet factories in 1992 who were interviewed by CWIN complained of frequent sexual abuse, including rape by adult co-workers, managers and brokers for the factories. According to children's rights advocates, underground brothels operate out of some of Nepal's carpet factories.

---

[10]*Misery Behind the* Looms, Child Workers in Nepal Concerned Center (CWIN), (Kathmandu: CWIN, May 1993), p.31. CWIN found that Tamangs, adults and children, constituted more than 80 percent of the total labor force in the carpet industry.

[11]*Action for Children*, Child Workers in Nepal Concerned Center, Issue No. 5, (Kathmandu, Nepal), June 1994, p.4.

[12]Interview with A.R. Panday, Chief District Officer of Nuwakot, Trisuli, Nuwakot District, Nepal, March 1994.

> [S]ome carpet factory brokers...roam in the villages to lure
> young girls to work in the carpet factories of Kathmandu where
> many of them are forced into prostitution and even trafficked to
> Bombay. These girls are abused and exploited by storekeepers,
> loom masters and checkers before they give up and agree to do
> the "night shifts." And they sell themselves for Rs.20-50 [0.40-
> $1.00] per trick. The customers are arranged by the pimps in the
> factory who take commissions from the girls. In Kathmandu's
> many garment factories, too, the girls do one kind of work
> during the day and another kind at night.[13]

The following cases of women interviewed by Human Rights Watch/Asia
demonstrate the link between the carpet industry and trafficking.

"Neela"

In 1989, when she was fourteen, "Neela's" stepfather took her from their
village in Sindhupalchowk to Bhaktapur, a suburb of Kathmandu, where a friend
of his got her a job in a carpet factory. A few months later, in January 1990, a
young male co-worker who had been introduced to Neela as her "cousin" suggested
that they leave the Bhaktapur factory and go to Kakarbhitta, a town on the Indian
border, where, he claimed, working conditions were better and they could earn
more money. Neela agreed, and was taken out of the factory by her stepfather, her
stepfather's friend and this young man. After six days, traveling by bus and by
train, they arrived in Bombay.

There, Neela was taken to the grounds of a temple where the men
introduced her to two women. She was told to go home with the women; the men
would join them later. Neela was taken to a house that she later discovered was the
home of the brothel manager. She stayed there overnight, and at 6:00 the next
morning she was taken to another house where sixteen or seventeen girls were
asleep on the floor. Because she was so young, Neela was taken to a
separate"training" room where she was kept for three months, after which she was
told she had been sold for Rs.15,000 [$500] and would have to work there until she
paid off her debt. Her first customer was a middle-aged man who paid Rs.5,000
[$166] for her because she was a virgin. Neela said the manager always charged
more money for new girls, but she was never told how much the regular customers

---

[13]Rupa Dita, "Child Prostitution in Nepal," *Voice of Child Workers*, Issue No. 15 and
16, (Kathmandu, Nepal), December 1992, p.57.

paid; all the money was given directly to the owner. Nor was she told how long it would take to repay her debt.

As the youngest in the brothel, Neela's treatment was better than for many of the girls and women working there. She was not beaten, even when she was caught trying to escape one night by pretending to go to the toilet which was outside behind the brothel. However, she was insulted and threatened, and saw others who worked there frequently beaten severely, "until blood came from their mouths," for trying to escape and for fighting.

Many other girls in the brothel were under-age and all were Nepali. Neela told Human Rights Watch/Asia that the brothel was frequently raided by police in search of underage girls and that when the police came, the brothel owners would try to hide the newcomers, because "not all police were the same." Sometimes police who came in civilian dress as paying customers and sought her out specifically would raid the brothel later.

Neela said condoms were not available in the brothel where she worked although customers sometimes brought their own. She never asked a customer to use a condom.

After about a year in the brothel Neela was picked up in a police raid and taken to an ashram, a shelter, for children because she was underage. In the ashram she tested positive for HIV. After two years there, when Neela was eighteen, the police asked her if she wanted to go home. She said she did, and the Indian police informed the Nepali police and she was taken to Kathmandu. She was brought first to Hanuman Dhoka police station in Kathmandu, then to Bhaktapur police station. She was held for eight days in Bhaktapur police detention. During that time the police took her to Teku Hospital[14] for an HIV test. She was not told the reason for the test; the police only told her that they were taking her for a check-up because she was returning from Bombay. Afterwards she was told she had tested positive for HIV. Neela said a journalist interviewed her just two days after she arrived in Kathmandu -- while she was still in police custody -- and her photo and story were published in a local paper, but she did not know which one. Because of this she decided not to try to locate her family. She now lives in a shelter.

Sanumaya Chaudhary
Sanumaya (Sanu) Chaudhary, age fifteen, was trafficked to India in 1991, also by a co-worker in a carpet factory, and rescued in January 1992. Her case was first published by the *Independent*, a Kathmandu-based English-language newspaper, in September 1992, soon after she lodged a complaint with the police

---

[14]The Nepal Ministry of Health's AIDS control program is located in Teku Hospital.

against a twenty-year-old woman who had taken her to India. Since then, Sanu's story has been reprinted by several organizations who worked with her.[15] Sanu's parents were migrants from Bara district in south-central Nepal who had come to Kathmandu to work in a carpet factory. Sanu's parents placed her in a small boarding school for destitute girls near the factory, but she was expelled for her suspected romantic involvement with the factory manager. Back in the carpet factory, Sanu, who had just turned fifteen, became friendly with an older girl who told her there were better paying jobs available in a carpet factory in Raxaul, just across the Indian border. The two girls talked it over with Sanu's parents and decided to go to Raxaul. Sanu took a only a change of clothes. She borrowed bus fare from her new friend.

After three days of traveling by bus and by train, the two girls arrived in a city Sanu thought was Raxaul. It turned out to be Bombay. The girls went directly to a building Sanu's companion said was the carpet factory and met the manager. Sanu was told she could have a bath; when she finished bathing, she found her friend had disappeared. Sanu was taken to a large room with five beds separated by curtains. She was given a nightgown and her clothes were taken away. Several older girls wearing thick make-up came into the room with men and drew the curtains behind them. The noise the couples made frightened Sanu. Then one of the men she had seen at the entrance to the building came into the room and ordered Sanu to go to bed with him. When she refused, he raped her and beat her for resisting. For the next week, Sanu was subjected to repeated rapes and beatings by brothel guards -- a "breaking in" period that is routine in many brothels. After a week of this abuse, she stopped fighting and began taking customers. Sanu was told she could leave the brothel when she repaid the Rs.50,000 [$1,666] the proprietor claimed had been paid to her parents.

"Santhi"
In addition to actual recruitment from the factories, false offers of employment in Nepal's carpet factories are a common ruse used to entice potential recruits. In an interview with Human Rights Watch/Asia in March 1994, "Santhi", age twenty-nine, told interviewers that after she was tricked into going to India by traffickers who offered her work in a carpet factory, she spent more than ten years in Bombay brothels before finally making her way back to Nepal. In Bombay, she contracted HIV.

Santhi, who returned to Nepal in 1991 after more than ten years in a series of brothels in Bombay, ran away from her home in Sindhupalchowk when she was

---

[15]"The Case of Sanu," *The Independent* (Kathmandu, Nepal), September 9, 1994.

a teenager. She went to Kathmandu where she first found work as a domestic servant. A male cousin came to Kathmandu to visit her and offered to help her get a job in a carpet factory in Birganj, a town on the Indian border. He told her that if she worked in the factory for two months she would begin earning a salary. Santhi left the house where she had been working and went with him. They travelled by bus, and then by train and then by taxi, going from Kathmandu to Birganj to Bombay. Midway, they were joined by an older man whom Santhi did not know.

When they reached Bombay they stopped in a park. Santhi was told to wait with her cousin. The older man left them in the park, and returned with a woman he introduced as his sister and said that they should go with her. They all got in a taxi and went to a house. Santhi was put in one room and the men were given another. That was the last time she saw them. Santhi found out later that a month after she arrived in Bombay, her cousin took her sister from their village and brought her to Bombay as well. Her sister and she were bought by the same person, but were kept in different brothels.

Marriage Offers

Fraudulent marriage offers are another common ruse employed by recruiters. In some cases, the traffickers actually go through a marriage ceremony. In others, the marriage offer itself is enough to lure a woman away from home. A police officer in Butwal told Human Rights Watch/Asia that in 1989 he arrested a very handsome youth in Jhapa district in eastern Nepal who had trafficked nine girls to Bombay by marrying them. He took each to Bombay and abandoned them in a crowd. An accomplice would then approach them, offer to help them find the missing young man and lead them to a brothel. The following case is typical of this kind of deception.

"Sita"

"Sita", thirty-one, returned from India in October 1993 after working for ten years in a Bombay brothel. She is a high-caste Hindu from a small village in Tanahu District, near Pokhara. Sita was married when she was fourteen. After two years of marriage, she became pregnant and her husband went to India in search of work. Her in-laws mistreated her so Sita returned to her parents' home. In 1983, when she was twenty and her son was four, a neighbor (who was also a relative and a close friend of Sita's) commented that Sita's husband had been gone a long time and probably was not coming back. She asked Sita if she would be willing to remarry, because there was a man from India who wanted to marry her.

Soon after, the neighbor came to the house and told Sita that the man from India was waiting for her on the bridge at the main road and that he wanted to elope. It was around noon; Sita told her family she was going to the fields to work and went instead to the bridge, perhaps ten minutes away. She brought her son with her.

The man was waiting for Sita as the neighbor had said. They caught a bus to Pokhara, the nearest town. In Pokhara he offered Sita a cigarette. Sita said she had learned to smoke from a friend in the village and so she took it. After smoking the cigarette, she remembers very little and thinks she may have passed out. Sita said she remembers boarding another bus and then waking up in a large cement room with a ceiling fan and three beds with curtains around them. The door was closed. There were six or seven other women in the room and she asked them where she was, but they spoke to her in a language she did not understand.

The man who brought her there took Sita's son and said he would show him around town. They never returned. Sita was frantic. She wanted to go out and search for them, but the owner, a woman from eastern Nepal, told her she had been sold to a brothel and could not leave. Sita never saw her son again.

Sita escaped to Nepal in October 1993 with the help of a Nepali vegetable seller she befriended in the brothel. Everyone in her village thought she was dead. When Sita returned to Nepal, she was afraid to go directly home -- worried her family would not accept her -- so she sent a message from Pokhara saying she had returned. It was the time of the Teej festival, when married daughters return to their home villages to visit their families. Everyone in the village came to the place where she was staying and hugged her and cried. Sita lives in her parents' home, where we were able to interview her. She says her family treats her well, because they know she was taken to India against her will. According to a lawyer familiar with her case, her brothers are less welcoming, and Sita may face problems when her elderly parents die.

Abductions

Simple abductions also occur, although they are less common than cases of fraud. Several women mentioned that they, or other women in the brothels where they worked, had been drugged by their abductors.

"Devi"

"Devi," age twenty-seven, lives with her parents in a small house in a village on the outskirts of Pokhara. She is a high-caste Hindu. Devi is married, but her estranged husband is said to be working in Korea, and she has not heard from him in years. Devi was trafficked to India in early June 1993. She returned to Nepal in December 1993. During that time, she was sold to three different brothels in less than four months because she refused customers and repeatedly tried to escape. When she finally did escape she worked in a textile factory for three months before the owner of the factory brought her home.

Devi was taken to India by neighbors, a mother and daughter, whom she knew quite well. They told her that they had to go to a market far from their village to pick up something and asked her to come along. Devi often went places with them, but usually they travelled by bus. That day there was a taxi waiting for them. They travelled a long way, and it was very late when they finally arrived in Badi Bazaar. They got in another taxi and arrived at a village house like her own. She was put in a room and the door was locked. Devi had no idea where she was.

A woman called Nithu told Devi that the woman she came with had gone out and would be back later, but she never came back. After three nights, Nithu made Devi travel with her by taxi and then train to another town. When Devi pleaded with her to let her go, she was told "No, you have been sold and have to work. All Nepali girls have to work."

Devi was taken to a room where she saw five girls from Pokhara whom she knew and four others. She asked the other girls there to help her escape, and eight days later when the brothel owner found out, Devi was sold to another brothel. After three or four days she attempted to escape again, this time by appealing to a Nepali client for help. She was overheard by another girl in the brothel who informed the owner. Devi was sold late that night to a third brothel. There were underage girls in all the brothels in which she worked. In the first two the average age was fifteen or sixteen. In the third brothel there were fifty girls and women of all ages; the two youngest were fourteen. Devi was never told how much the first two owners paid for her. The last owner told her she had paid Rs.40,000 [$1,333] for her and that she would have to work it off.

"Kamala"

"Kamala", age twenty-six, returned to Nepal in September 1993 after spending nine years in India. She was drugged and abducted by her stepfather's elder brother and his son and trafficked to India when she was seventeen. Kamala had been visiting her uncle and his three children, who lived in Biratnager, a town very near the Indian border. Once when she was visiting he suggested that they make a trip to Jogvani. The uncle, his wife and eldest son went along. Along the way they stopped for tea. Kamala was given milk. The milk smelled bad, but she drank it anyway. The next thing she remembers is waking up slightly on a train and then perhaps again in a taxi. When she really woke up she was in a big hall with a lot of lights, which turned out to be a hotel lobby, but she does not know the name of the hotel.

Her cousin and uncle were with her. They told her that they needed to go to the bank and left her alone in the hotel lobby. While they were gone Kamala overheard two men speaking Hindi; they were talking about taking someone to a brothel. She asked the men what they were talking about and who they were taking to a brothel. She asked where her relatives had gone. The men told her she had been sold. She started to cry and said that it was impossible, she did not believe it. They asked her if she could read and when she said she could (she had studied up to the seventh standard), they showed her a receipt for Rs.40,000.

The hotel owner told her that this was not the first time her uncle and cousin had brought girls there. They had brought two other girls previously -- one was Nepali, one looked Indian and was from the Terai.

The men tried to put her in a taxi. She said she had to go to the toilet first and a small boy showed her where it was. She locked herself in and would not come out. She said she was able to lock herself in because the hotel owner did not know she was there and there were a number of stalls, so she hid. That was at about 9:00 P.M. She hid in the toilet until about 4:00 A.M. By then she was sure the men had given up. She slipped out of the hotel and escaped. She was taken in by a woman who lived in a nearby slum who got her a job as a domestic servant in the home of a couple who worked at a hospital. But as is the case with many domestic workers, her employers "held" her salary for her so that when she left their service, she had no money. It took Kamala nine years working as a domestic servant in two different households to make her way back to Nepal.

The Routes

The trafficking industry in Nepal is remarkable not only because it represents the work of large and well-organized criminal gangs and preys on very young victims, but also because the villages from which girls and women are trafficked are so remote. Most are far from the nearest road. Much of the journey from the hill villages to Kathmandu, which can take more than two days, must be covered on foot over rugged mountain paths. Villagers say that despite this, it is not uncommon for traffickers to travel these paths on nights with a full moon with several girls in tow. Police intervention is extremely rare. From their villages, girls are first taken to Kathmandu, either to guest houses or carpet factories, and from there to border towns like Birganj, Kakarbhitta, Bhairawaha or Biratnagar where they are sold to brokers. The going rate is said to be about one thousand Nepali rupees [$20].

Girls abducted from the Terai and eastern Nepal are usually taken directly to the border. The brokers then travel by bus or by train to India -- to Bombay, Calcutta, Delhi or to smaller cities -- and sell these girls to a brothel owner or madam for up to Rs.50,000 [$1,666]. According to researchers in Kathmandu, most brokers travel by local bus to Delhi, and then by bus or train to Bombay. Buses, they say, are preferred because they are less obvious than trains.

Local police in Birganj told Human Rights Watch/Asia that although their town was a well-known border crossing for traffickers, the routes change frequently:

> Lately, the girls have changed their route. Now they go through Gaur and Thori (to the east and west of Birganj respectively), two places with minimal Nepali customs and some Indian customs police who are not very vigilant.

Activists note that trafficking routes also appear to be changing with migration to the Terai. While there is still much trafficking from the hills of the Bagmati zone, as families migrate in search of work, more girls are being sold from urban areas and villages along the highways.

IN THE BROTHELS

Nepali women in India's red-light areas remain largely segregated in brothels located in what are known to their Indian counterparts and their customers as "Nepali *kothas*" or compounds. The concentrations of Nepalis vary from city to city, but appear to be highest in the Bombay neighborhood of Kamathipura. Brothels vary by size, physical configuration, ethnicity of sex workers, and price. But in all cases, movement outside the brothels is strictly controlled, and inmates are subjected to both psychological and physical abuse. The cheapest brothels, nothing more than dark, claustrophobic rooms with cloth dividers hung between the beds, are known among Nepalis as "pillow houses." About one-fifth of all Bombay's brothel workers, or approximately 20,000 women, work in squalid brothels like these on numbered lanes (or *gallis*) in Kamathipura. Certain lanes, like the 11th and the 13th, are known particularly as Nepali gallis.[16] Many customers seek out Nepali prostitutes specifically, because of their looks and their exotic reputations.

The segregation of Nepali girls and women in these gallis exposes them to a wider range of clients, and a wider and more unpredictable range of sexual expectations, treatment, and disease. Nepalis are sought out by customers who think their "golden" skin make them more attractive. Brothel owners say Nepalis' faces and bodies stay youthful longer. The Nepalis also suffer from a reputation of sexual compliance among both Indian sex workers and customers, who say Nepalis engage in higher-risk sexual acts, such as anal intercourse and sado-masochistic sex, than their Indian counterparts, who may have more control over the terms of sexual contact. Consequently, kotha managers and their clients view Nepali women in prostitution as a special case, and madams routinely receive special requests for Nepalis. Foreigners from outside India, particularly the Middle East, are also said to view Nepalis as special within the sex industry.

Most girls and women start out in these cheap brothels where they are "broken in" through a process of rapes and beatings. They are frequently then resold to other brothels where they can bring in more money for the owner. Some women are also resold as punishment for escape attempts. An activist in Nepal who has counselled many returned prostitutes related what he knew of the Indian brothel system.

> There are several grades of prostitutes, based on beauty, hard work, "talent." The top are call girls. Then comes "bungalow," which is a higher grade of regular brothel, then comes "pillow house," which is the lowest. Most girls start out in pillow house and work up if they do well....Some girls receive training, how to approach customers, languages. During training girls are beaten and locked in a room like a jail, but a very small one, until they stop fighting. At first a girl gets two or three clients a day, then it escalates.... In pillow house girls can have as many as forty customers a day. But they earn no money until they have

---

[16]Some activists in Bombay's red-light districts believe that the auspicious number "7" in the building number, often attached to a neon sign saying, "Welcome," also signifies a Nepali kotha. Accordingly, this "welcome system" is designed to highlight the segregation that already exists, and to attract customers with a special preference for Nepalis.

paid off their debt. After they have paid off their debt, one part
of their earnings goes to gharwali, one part to "local taxes," and
one part to herself.

It is one or two years before a girl is allowed out of the brothel
and then, after they have confidence she won't try to escape, she
is allowed to go to the cinema or shopping with a guard from the
brothel....If a girl manages to escape, she is illiterate, she knows
nothing about the city. She will fall victim to local people or the
police.

Both psychological and physical means are used to "break in" new girls
purchased for the brothels. Indian activist Preeti Pai Patkar of the organization
Prerana (inspiration), which works for Bombay sex workers' rights, told Human
Rights Watch/Asia that there were special interior lanes in areas like Falkland Road
in Bombay where rooms and even whole buildings were maintained especially for
torturing newly-procured women. Younger girls and children are reportedly hidden
in attic spaces in these buildings.

Psychological abuse, threats and intimidation are an integral part of the
process and are used exclusively with girls who are purchased as virgins and can
therefore be sold for higher prices if their "training" does not include rape. This
psychological abuse continues well beyond the first customer, however, with
brothel staff using conflicting messages to break down the victim's resistance and
build dependency. A common tactic involves certain brothel staff treating the
victim abusively, telling her repeatedly that she is dirty or defiled, for example,
while another -- often the gharwali herself -- consoles her and tells her that she is
among family.[17]

When the psychological approach does not work, the brothel staff resorts
to physical abuse, or allows customers to do so. This abuse can include beatings,
gang rapes, and torture with burning cigarettes.

---

[17]Typically, the "consoler," perhaps a senior woman in the brothel who has been
through the ordeal herself, will say something like, "You are like my daughter - you are
suffering just like me."

Debt Bondage

Debt bondage, prohibited under The Supplementary Convention on the Abolition of Slavery, the Slave Trade and Institutions and Practices Similar to Slavery, is defined as a situation in which debtors pledge their personal services against a debt they owe, but the person to whom they owe it fails to deduct the value of their services from the debt, or the length and nature of those services are not respectively limited and defined.[18] The debt bondage which supports the trafficking nexus is also tantamount to forced labor, defined by the ILO as, "All work or service which is exacted from any person under the menace of any penalty and for which the said person has not offered himself voluntarily." Slavery and forced labor are prohibited by other international law[19] and under Nepali and Indian laws. India enacted the Bonded Labour System (Abolition) Act in 1976 which outlaws all forms of bonded and slave labor. In addition, article 374 of the Indian Penal Code makes it a crime to compel unlawfully any person to labor against his or her will.

Every Nepali girl or woman with whom we spoke said that the brothel owner or manager forced her to work by invoking her indebtedness. This supposed debt, and the threats and beatings that accompanied it, were the major obstacles between her and the possibility of freedom. For most of the women interviewed, the debt was the amount of money the brothel owner said she paid a broker when the girl was purchased, plus the costs of medical care and protection money or payoffs to police and local thugs. Men interviewed in Nepal who were familiar with the brothel system said the girls were also charged 10 percent interest on their purchase price.

The Delhi-based welfare organization, Bharatiya Patita Udhar Sabha, charged in a 1993 letter to the Home Minister that some madams in Delhi even compelled girls to sign forms stating that they were voluntarily working as maid servants and also as bonded laborers until they repaid the loans they had purportedly undertaken. Although occasionally the gharwali may pay for food, clothes and medicine, these costs are frequently added to the debts. In any case, a girl's indebtedness to the gharwali is based on the gharwali's own expenses. For example, a gharwali who has paid Rs.15,000 [$500] to purchase a girl, plus an additional Rs.5,000 [$166] to the police so she will not be arrested under the

---

[18]Supplementary Convention on the Abolition of Slavery, Section I, Article 1; 1957.

[19]Universal Declaration, Article 4 and International Covenant on Civil and Political Rights, Article 8.

Immoral Traffic in Persons Prevention Act of 1986 (ITPPA), would calculate the girl's "debt" at Rs. 20,000 [$666], plus interest. The owners then take one hundred percent of her earnings until that amount is paid off.

A woman's earnings depend on the type of brothel in which she is employed, her age and appearance, and the nature of the sex acts she is compelled to perform. Devi said that all the women and girls where she worked were dependent on tips for food to supplement the meager meals provided by the brothel, but that as a newcomer without regular customers, and an older woman at that, she got few tips. Devi told Human Rights Watch/Asia that although she was never allowed to handle any money in the pillow houses where she worked, she heard from other women that the owners charged Rs.30 [$1] for five minutes. In the bungalow, where she took the money from customers beforehand and turned it over to the management, the rate was Rs.110 [$3.66], again for a very short time.

A villager in Nuwakot district who had travelled to Bombay several times told Human Rights Watch/Asia that in his experience a typical pillow house charged Rs.50 [$1.66] for fifteen minutes, and that a woman earned between Rs.1500-2500 [$50-83] a day which she turned over to the owner. In a day she might have more than twenty-five customers and she could earn small tips of Rs. 2-5 [five to fifteen cents] from customers. A bungalow-style brothel charged about Rs.100 [$3.33] for an hour and the girls kept the tips.

Although most business is conducted in the brothel, and is charged by the minute or hour, customers can pay extra to take women outside.[20] For Rs. 500-1000 [$16-$33] a girl will be sent to a client's house or a hotel for the night. If a customer buys a woman's services for a longer period her debt resumes upon her return. For example, one Bombay customer paid Rs.12,000 [$400] and kept a woman in his home for two weeks. He returned her to the brothel, where she worked to repay the remaining debt.

A girl who has managed to escape, but finds that she has no way to support herself may negotiate her return to a gharwali, resulting in a fifty-fifty division of her earnings. Sometimes the woman attaches herself to a local thug to support her in her negotiations with the gharwali. However, this type of an agreement frequently results in indebtedness of a different sort, since the girl is often convinced to take a loan from the gharwali to see herself through.

---

[20]In the evenings, informants described jeeps full of girls heading toward the suburbs of Bombay, en route to beer halls, restaurants, clubs, and hotels. Although the streets are lined with police, they rarely interfere.

None of the Nepali girls or women we interviewed knew about the monetary arrangements between the brothel owner, the agents and their families. Because the women did not know how much money had been exchanged or how much they earned, they did not know the amount of their debt. But all were frequently reminded that they had to work to pay off their debts, and many were threatened or beaten for not earning enough.

> • "Santhi" said she worked in three low-grade brothels or "pillow houses" and one fancier brothel commonly called a "bungalow." In the pillow house she had fifteen to twenty customers a day and, except for regulars, customers paid Rs.15 [50 cents] for five minutes. She also worked for four months in a bungalow which charged Rs.100-Rs.300 [$3-$10] per hour. Some customers would pay to take the girls out all night, or sometimes for days at a time. If they were taken out to a hotel they were paid at least Rs.1,000 [$33.]. Although Santhi does not know how much she was originally sold for, she was told that each time she was sold it was for a higher price. None of the owners ever told her how much she had to repay, but the brothel managers kept track of how many customers each girl served per day and claimed to figure that against their debt.

Some of the women had a vague understanding that they would have to work for a specific length of time to pay off the debt, and that there was an agreed-upon amount of payment given at the end of the time. We were told both by returnees from brothels and other people from their villages that there were rules in Bombay brothels about how long girls should work and how much they would be paid. But although this was a persistent rumor, none of the girls we spoke with earned anything like the amounts typically mentioned, or knew anyone who had.[21]

> • "Santhi" had heard there was a rule that the brothel can keep you three years, but after three years they have to give you Rs.20,000 [$666], gold and clothes. But they did not give her

---

[21]A villager we interviewed in Sikharbeshi said he had heard that a women's group in Bombay has gotten agreement from brothel owners that after a girl has worked eight years, she should get Rs.20,000 [$666], a box of clothes and a certain amount of gold. Within those first eight years, all the money is taken by the gharwali. If she goes back after eight years, the money is supposed to be split fifty-fifty with the gharwali.

anything like that. Most of the money she brought out with her was her tips, and she managed to send a box of clothes to her father. After she was there seven years, her father came to see her, but the owner said she had to stay another two years before she could leave. After two more years, her father came to the brothel and brought her out. When she left the brothel she was given Rs.5,000 [$166] which she turned over to her father.

• "Sita" was told that she had to pay off her purchase price of Rs.20,000 [$666], and that was used to force her to work when she did not want to. She worked in the same brothel for ten years and was never told she had paid off her debt.[22] She told Human Rights Watch/Asia, "Nobody was allowed to leave after four years like people say they are." Sita had no idea what the brothel charged her customers because the money was given to the owner. She had nine or ten customers a day and worked from 10 A.M. to 11 P.M. Sometimes customers gave the girls tips, which they were allowed to keep. The owner provided one meal a day and they had to pay for the second meal with their tip money. They also had to pay for clothes and make-up with tip money they saved. The owner paid for treatment at a private clinic when they were sick, and added it to their debt. They received injections once a month, but Sita did not know what they were for, and they were given pills to induce abortions. The price of the monthly injections was also added to their debt.

According to "Maya," brothel inmates got about five days leave after an abortion before they had to start working again. One woman she knew had aborted

---

[22]If Sita served nine men a night, assuming a twenty-eight-day working month (a conservative estimate since Sita was allowed no days off for menstruation), and the going rate at her brothel was Rs.50 per client, the gross income for the brothel owner from her work alone would be Rs.12,600 ($420) a month. If Sita had been getting one third of the income, and her debt remained steady, she should have been able to repay her debt of Rs.20,000 in five months. If, as was the case for many of the girls, the debt was increased by ten percent to include "interest," she still should have been able to repay it in less than six months. But Sita worked in the same brothel for ten years, and never earned her release.

twice. The cost of abortions, plus interest, was added to the debt. One owner said that the abortions had cost her Rs.1,000 [$33] each time and then charged interest on top of it, increasing the woman's debt by Rs.4,000 [$133].

In addition to the money earned by parents from the sale of their daughters (a few hundred rupees if she is sold to a local recruiter, or several thousand if the family sells her directly to a broker), male relatives also make periodic trips to India to collect the girls' earnings. In villages in places like Nuwakot and Sindhupalchowk, if a village has several women in Bombay brothels, a prominent member of the village may be appointed to travel to India, collect the money they earn and bring it back to their parents. For the girls, this means that not only are they under pressure to pay off their debt to the brothel owner, but out of whatever earnings they do receive, in the form of tips primarily, they are expected to help support their families.

Illegal Confinement

There are other aspects of the work in brothels which reinforce its non-voluntary nature. One of these is illegal confinement. Debt bondage is enforced by the near total confinement of the women and girls to the brothel premises. Women and girls are generally not allowed to leave the brothel or its immediate surroundings without escorts and are threatened with a range of consequences, including arrest by the Indian police or capture by other brothel owners, should they attempt to do so. The women and girls we interviewed explained that they would be beaten severely if they tried to escape.[23]

With few exceptions, the Nepali women are unable to communicate with anyone outside of the brothel and some are even forbidden to take Nepali clients out of fear that the latter might be more likely to help the women escape. Even conversation with customers is sometimes forbidden. A villager in Nuwakot who was familiar with Bombay's brothels told Human Rights Watch/Asia, "Only girls who pay off their 'loan,' have gone on a holiday to their village and come back, are allowed to leave the brothel alone. Before that they are not allowed out alone."

In Sita's case, no one in the brothel was allowed to go out unescorted. Everything was brought by vendors into the brothel to sell -- food, clothes, even

[23]Article 8 of the ICCPR states that: "1. No one shall be held in slavery; slavery and the slave-trade in all their forms shall be prohibited. 2. No one shall be held in servitude. 3. (a) No one shall be required to perform forced or compulsory labour. Article 9 guarantees the right to liberty and security of person.

videos. They were allowed no contact with their families. Sita, who could not read or write herself, said that none of the women in the brothel were permitted to write or to have pens and paper. Santhi also stated that the girls in her brothels were never allowed out for fear they would run away. Everything was brought to the house, and shopkeepers charged very high prices.

None of the interviewees were in regular communication with their families, none were from villages with telephones and several were illiterate. One woman was lucky enough to find a customer who was willing to send word to her family. A Nepali man she met in the brothel wrote a letter to her family telling them what had happened to her, and her brother went to Bombay to try and see her there, but he was not allowed to do so. Her family then brought charges against her trafficker, who was arrested and then released on bail after a month and a half. The case was proceeding, but she was not informed of its progress.

Fear of beatings, arrest or recapture by other brothel agents keeps many girls from trying to escape. Devi stated that the brothel had a window so that all the girls could be observed by the management. When she was seen trying to escape, she was beaten. Whenever there was a police raid the owner would hide all the girls; those who tried to come out would be beaten.   Devi said that only newcomers tried to run away; the older ones would not try to escape. "Maybe they know that those who run away would be sold to another brothel by men on the street, so they don't run." The girls were also afraid of the police. In September or October 1993, a girl who had escaped was taken into custody and raped by the police. The next day the police brought her back to the brothel and told the owner to bring out all the new girls and leave only the "licensed" ones. The owner gave the police Rs.10,000 [$333,] and they went away.

Working Conditions

Tips provide the only source of income for most newcomers to the brothels. Without tips, girls are entirely dependent on the brothel owner for food, sometimes only one meal a day, and the women have to supplement the meager food and clothing provided by the brothel by using their own tips. Most owners permit girls to keep tips, which amount to only a few rupees per customer, but in some cases even this avenue of earning is restricted.

> • For the first two or three years "Santhi" was in the brothels she was forbidden to ask for tips. In one house where she worked, the girls were supposed to give the owner any tips they received.

They were made to swear in front of the brothel altar that they would not keep tips from customers. But Santhi said the brothel owner provided only one meal a day, in the morning, and girls would secretly hoard their tip money to pay for an evening meal. Sometimes customers would bring them special food, like chicken, which was a treat because meat in the brothel was very rare. But they had to hide the food or the owner would become angry. In one brothel where Santhi worked, girls were only allowed to sleep in a bed if they had a customer, otherwise they slept on the floor.

● "Devi" did not get many tips because newcomers got fewer regular customers. The brothel owner provided them with two meals a day, but the food was not very good. With tips they could buy tea and snacks.

● "Sita's" owner gave the women in her brothel one meal a day. They had to pay for the second meal. They also had to pay for clothes and make-up. For all these things they would save up their tips, and buy from vendors who would come to the brothels and who charged very high prices.

None of the women interviewed by Human Rights Watch/Asia was allowed to refuse customers. In some cases they were not even allowed to speak to them. Their days were spent waiting in line for customers or serving them, and they were beaten and humiliated for refusing.

In the bungalow where Devi worked, the girls stood or sat in a row in their make-up and the customers, who also stood in a queue, chose the girl they wanted. They were given only a very short time with each customer and sometimes, if customers tried to ask newcomers too many questions, they ran out of time before they had time to have sex. If the owner found out that a customer had been asking a new girl about herself, the girl would be beaten. In the pillow houses in which Devi worked, the day started at 8:00 A.M. and they worked until late at night. In the bungalow, the day started at 4:00 P.M. and went until 2:00 A.M. The girls were expected to stand or sit in line the entire time, whether or not there were customers. They were given no time off, even when they were menstruating. Devi said the happier you made the owners, the nicer they were to you, so sometimes if she was menstruating she took the customer's money first and then told him she was menstruating. If she was lucky, he would go away. Girls very rarely refused a customer, because those who refused were beaten.

Sita also said the women in her brothel were not allowed to refuse customers. They were made to sit in a room and the customers would choose the girl they wanted. If the girls refused, they were hit and verbally abused by the owner in front of the customer: "If you won't go, maybe your mother will."

Besides being compelled to serve customers, brothel owners sometimes force workers to perform personal housework or childcare chores. Santhi said that the brothel madams lived in separate rooms with their husbands and children. Santhi and the others were sent to clean these rooms. Every Saturday they had to clean the room, wash the family's clothes and bathe the children. Devi said that besides sleeping with customers, the women and girls in the brothels were expected to do housework for the owner, including washing the floors at the owner's house and doing her laundry, which they brought to the brothel to wash.

IV. THE ROLE OF THE NEPALI AND INDIAN GOVERNMENTS

Despite the fact that both Nepal and India have numerous laws criminalizing trafficking and prescribing severe penalties for abusers, trafficking in women and girls flourishes between the two countries. Human Rights Watch/Asia's investigation reveals the involvement of police and other government officials at various points along the trafficking routes, but there has been little effort on the part of either government to investigate charges of official complicity or to punish those responsible.

Police demand bribes as payment for not arresting traffickers and brothel owners, or are themselves involved in trafficking. Government officials protect traffickers who are politically influential.

POLICE CORRUPTION AND COMPLICITY

The Bharatiya Patita Udhar Sabha, in its letter to the Home Minister in 1993, charged that police regularly extorted large sums of money in red-light areas in the name of protection -- up to Rs. 26,000 [$866] per day in Delhi alone. The organization president, Khairati Lal Bhola, complained that out of the Rs.55 [$1.83] paid by a customer in one of the city's better brothels, Rs.10 [.33] went to the police. On a daily basis, he charged, the local police station received cuts according to rank: a constable could expect Rs.25 [$.83], a head constable received Rs.40 [$1.33], and an Assistant Sub-Inspector (ASI) received Rs.80 to Rs.100 [$2.66-$3.33]. The groups charged that the Station House Officer (SHO) received Rs.500 [$16.66] per month, and the district special branch police, which addresses special categories of crimes, collected monthly payments of about Rs.300 [$10] per *kotha* [brothel compound] of ten girls, and Rs.500 [$16.66] for larger kothas.[1]

In the case of recently trafficked girls and women, the organization charged that police were involved in the staged process called "registering" the victims. In this process, the madam would notify the police of the arrival of a new victim in her establishment and pay a bribe for their silence. The madam routinely paid between Rs.5000 and Rs.25,000 [$166-$833] to the police station on scale with her purchase price. In the case of a minor, the police took their bribe from the

---

[1]*The Statesman* (Delhi, India), August 30, 1993; *The Pioneer* (Delhi, India), December 30, 1993.

madam, kept the girl for a day in lock-up, and produced her in court the next day along with a falsified First Information Report (FIR) attesting to her adult status, thereby protecting the brothel owner from any future charges related to the prostitution of a minor. The released minor girl, newly registered with the authorities as twenty-one years of age or older, would be handed back to the madam. For this service, the madam paid the police Rs. 500 to Rs. 1000. [$16-$33] Sometimes the girl was given falsified papers and brought before the magistrate on a trumped-up charge of seduction in a public place, and handed back to the madam on payment of a fine of about Rs. 1000 [$33] for her release. Thus, for a fee, the madam is assured of police collusion in keeping the trafficking victim captive, while the performance of a few legal routines protects the police from complaints of negligence.

In the words of one Indian journalist:

> The entry of Nepalese girls into the flesh market is an ingeniously conceived mouse-trap. The exchange of money takes place under the eyes of the girl. A pimp in the G.B. Road area was fairly glib about it. "The money is paid to the concerned area's cops for registering an FIR (so that if the girl is a minor, her age is entered as 18 officially), and a fine of Rs. 1,000 is paid to the magistrate for her release -- the charge is fabricated as seduction in a public place."

This total cost of the transaction, including a heavy packet for the police -- is entered by the "madam" of the brothel in her ever-thickening notebook as "karz" (debt) on the girl, which she will, through selling her body, repay along with 10 percent interest. Thus, she has to work for five or six years in the brothel as no-wage worker, after which she can save and send back home something.[2]

The testimony of Devi, Tara and other women interviewed by Human Rights Watch/Asia supported charges of police collusion with pimps and brothel owners to profit from the trafficking and arrest of minor girls. Judging from Devi's testimony, the Bombay police also appear to participate in a similar "registration" or "licensing" charade to that described in Delhi's red-light areas.

---

[2]*Hindustan Times*, "The Nightmare Continues; Pankaj Tuli on the Sad Plight of Young Nepalese Girls who are Lured into India and Forced into Prostitution," March 20, 1994.

Bharatiya Patita Udhar Sabha also charged that to set up a new brothel, large amounts of money ranging from Rs. 50,000 [$1,666] and Rs. 200,000 [$6,666] had to be paid to the police. The purchase of a new kotha of fifty or more inmates by a well-to-do owner required a police payoff of about Rs. 300,000 [$10,000].[3]

While they know that police corruption occurs, the trafficking victims themselves are often kept in the dark about the details of these transactions. "Padma" said she thought that the Criminal Investigation Department (CID) at Marwari Chowk and Dilli Darbar (neighborhood police stations in Bombay) were each paid Rs. 60 per month. She said that CID cars came by the brothel every five or six months, and that fines of Rs.100 [$3.33] had to be paid by the brothel keeper for each girl they picked up in order to get them released.

The "Tulasa case" of 1982, which involved the rescue of a young Nepali girl who was abducted into the brothels of Bombay and subsequently infected with multiple sexually-transmitted diseases, first revealed to the general Indian public the extent of police complicity in trafficking from Nepal into India. In 1982, a thirteen-year-old girl, Tulasa, was abducted by an acquaintance from her home village of Thankut, near Kathmandu, and smuggled into Bombay via the border town of Birganj. She was beaten into submission by the acquaintance and his colleagues. She was sold to three different brothels in Bombay, at prices ranging from Rs. 5,000 to Rs. 7,500. In addition to the sex work she was forced to do in the brothel at a minimum of three customers per night, she was sent to various city hotels to entertain mostly Arab customers, for Rs.180 a night. The abuse of the girl continued until she collapsed with three venereal diseases and tuberculosis. Rescue efforts began when she was brought to Bombay's J.J. Hospital for treatment in November 1982. At the hospital, Tulasa was given police protection against possible reprisals from the prostitution industry. After a period of stay in the Dongri Remand Home, she returned to Nepal to take up residence in the Cheshire Home for the disabled in Jorpatti. Doctors evaluated Tulasa and found her to be severely damaged physically and psychologically. Over the years, she remained incoherent and rambling in her speech. She was confined to a wheelchair and complained that her stomach hurt all the time, and that she could not go to the toilet. Her family no longer visited her. In 1994 Tulasa broke her leg in a suicide attempt.

---

[3]*The Statesman* (Delhi, India), August 30, 1993; *The Pioneer* (Delhi, India), December 1993.

Tulasa's story supported what everyone in the business understood as the norm: police were involved in the highly organized and systematic business of trafficking. One of the leaders of the team that rescued Tulasa, Dr. I.S.Gilada of the Indian Health Organisation (IHO), noted the help of the then Police Commissioner and the local police station in the arrest of thirty-two persons -- including three brothel owners -- implicated in Tulasa's ordeal, and concluded that the police had known all along what was transpiring in the trafficking industry.[4]

The IHO's records on the Tulasa case demonstrate the longevity of several patterns of trafficking which Human Rights Watch/Asia has documented in Nepal and India to date, notably: abduction carried out on home ground in Nepal, violence used to break down the trafficking victim, exchange of money at all levels of trafficking transactions, victim's high-level exposure to disease and lack of medical treatment, and complicity of police and other governmental authorities at various levels in Nepal as well as in India.

Activists attribute the successful prosecution and stiff penalties given in Tulasa's case to the wide publicity accompanying her rescue and rehabilitation. Tulasa's abductors were given twenty years in prison. Following the public outcry, the governments of India and Nepal signed a 1985 cooperation agreement addressing the rescue and repatriation of Nepali girls trafficked into brothels in India.[5]

---

[4] *Illustrated Weekly of India* (Bombay, India), July 17-23, 1993.

[5] While there continues to be some official cooperation between Indian and Nepali police regarding the return of Nepali women from India, implementation has been uneven. Much of the contact between the two forces appears to be quite *ad hoc*; several police officers and women interviewed in Nepal thought returns happened most often because a particularly compassionate officer in India took it upon himself to help a woman get home, and that this was done informally, sometimes at the officer's expense. In general, police on Nepal's border seemed confused about the rules governing their contact with Indian police. One officer thought Indian police could only enter Nepal if they were out of uniform. Another said this wasn't so, that uniformed police crossed the border frequently. Both said that Indian police (in or out of uniform) sometimes took women all the way back to their home villages, although it was more common for women to be delivered to the Nepali border police.

THE RESPONSE OF THE COURTS

The Indian courts have occasionally recognized official complicity in the sex trade. For example, in February 1994, a division bench of the Supreme Court found two police officers -- Additional Superintendent of Police Pratap Singh and Circle Officer B. K. Chaturvedi -- in Uttar Pradesh guilty of contempt for disobeying the court's December 1993 order to rescue a twenty-year-old woman named Nasreen from a local red-light area after it had been shown that her husband had sold her into prostitution, and that she had been kept captive with police collusion. Two other police officers, Senior Superintendent of Police R. N. Kataria and Sub-Inspector Prempal Singh, were ordered to show cause for lying to the court. The court also warned the police against intimidating and harassing Nasreen's family, which had filed the initial complaint. Nasreen's mother had contended that the police refused to act when she first approached them, and in fact one officer demanded a bribe of Rs. 4,000 before throwing her out of the police station. Court proceedings showed that the police colluded in moving Nasreen out of the red-light area and across state lines until the Supreme Court ordered that she be produced. Chief Justice M.N. Venkatachalliah was reported to have opined that harassment "seems to be the police culture," and expressed determination to impose "constitutional culture on the police force." However, the court did let off several police officers and constables on their unconditional apology, including Senior Superintendent of Police Mr. Jamal Ashraf, Deputy Superintendent of Police S. N. Singh, and Inspector S. N. Yadav.[6]

In the November 1993 disposal of a twelve-year-old case, Justice G. N. Ray of the Indian Supreme Court noted that important local politicians were involved in trafficking in the Morena-Dholpur zone which falls in three states, Uttar Pradesh, Madhya Pradesh, and Rajasthan. The case under review had been filed ten years earlier, when a journalist proved the ease with which women could be bought and sold by purchasing a woman called Kamala and subsequently writing about it. At the time, the deputy inspector general of the Criminal Investigation Department had submitted a report in which he had asked that sympathetic police officers posted in the sex market areas ought to be given an assurance that they would not be transferred out for at least three years. The report maintained that this was necessary to prevent interference in the police officers'

---

[6]*The Hindu* (Madras, India), February 4, 1994; *Deccan Herald*, (Bangalore, India), February 9, 1994; *Indian Express* (Bombay, India), February 11, 1994; *Times of India* (Bombay, India), February 15, 1994.

work from politicians and other influential persons who were involved in the sex trade.[7]

POLICE RAIDS IN INDIA

Activists and trafficked women told Human Right Watch/Asia that although police harassment of commercial sex workers in Bombay was commonplace, the Bombay police rarely undertook formal raids or "rescues" in the city's red-light districts. Activist Preeti Pai Patkar said that when these raids did occur, they appeared to be made to fulfil police quotas or to carry out political vendettas. She thought international pressure also sometimes led to raids, but that on the whole women in prostitution were viewed as criminals by the police and by society at large and were not thought worthy of extra rescue efforts.

Police in Bombay maintained that they did conduct regular raids on brothels, although high-level criminal cases took precedence.[8] But most law enforcement against prostitution appears to be aimed at the arrest of individual sex workers for solicitation and other public offenses, rather than against traffickers, brothels owners or pimps. A press report from March 1993 estimated that more than forty women were charged every week under Section 110 of the Bombay Police Act in the jurisdiction of the Victoria Terminus Railway Station for misbehavior in a public place.[9] Figures for the total number of brothel raids and prosecutions of individuals for trafficking and brothel keeping have not been made public by Bombay's Vigilance Cell [vice squad] since the mid-1980s, but statistics in a widely-referred-to study by sociologist Jean D'Cunha in 1986 indicated that between 1980 and 1985, almost six times as many women were arrested for soliciting and "indecent behavior" as men or women were for trafficking, pimping or running brothels. According to police records, during that five-year period, 44,663 women were arrested for "indecent behavior" under Section 110(b) of the Bombay Police Act, and an estimated 7,600 were arrested under Sections 7 and 8

---

[7]*Times of India*, (Bombay) November 26, 1993.

[8] A police official interviewed by Human Rights Watch/Asia in September 1994 claimed that the Bombay police were still too busy investigating a series of bombings that occurred on March 12, 1993, to spare attention to trafficking or prostitution, consequently reducing the manpower available for searches and raids of brothels.

[9]*Indian Express* (Bombay), March 1, 1993.

of the Suppression of Immoral Traffic in Women and Girls Act of 1956 (SITA) which prohibit soliciting and prostitution "in or near a public place." (Of those arrests, 6,845 were confirmed by the authorities; statistics for women arrested under Section 8(b) for 1980 were not available, but the average number of arrests per year for the following four years was 830.)[10] In contrast, of the 409 brothel keepers arrested between 1981 and 1985, only two were convicted. One was fined Rs. 150 or one day of rigorous imprisonment; the other was fined Rs. 10. In all, 469 brothel keepers and 1,116 pimps were arrested between 1980 and 1985 under SITA and the Bombay Police Act respectively; 304 "procurers" were also arrested under SITA between 1980 and 1984.[11]

A female police officer in the Women-in-Distress Cell of the Bombay headquarters of the CID, who had participated as an accompanying officer on three brothel raids between 1992 and 1994, described the "rescue" process to a Human Rights Watch/Asia researcher. She said that on an average of once or twice a month, a customer came to police headquarters to report that he had encountered a girl who wished to escape from a brothel. After approaching the Women-in-Distress Cell with his story, he would be taken upstairs to Vigilance Cell officials to make a statement. The customer would then be asked to accompany the police on the "rescue." As a matter of procedure, police undertaking such a raid would formally ask the girls and women they approached if they wished to continue in the business, or if they wanted to go home to their families. The officer noted that minors approached by police generally wished to go home, as did adult women from other parts of India, notably South India. But she observed that most Nepali women she encountered did not wish to return to Nepal.[12] The reasons given by Nepali women and activists to the Human Rights Watch/Asia researcher were similar to those given to the police officer during raids: the Nepali women felt

---

[10]Section 8 prohibits "seducing or soliciting for the purpose of prostitution" in or within sight of a public place. 8(a) proscribes the use of "words, gestures," or exposure of person (and specifics such acts as "sitting by a window or on the balcony of a building") in order to attract customers for prostitution. 8(b) covers loitering, solicitation ,and other acts which "cause obstruction or annoyance...or offend against public decency..."

[11]Jean D'Cunha (1986), quoted in C.P. Sujaya, "Women, Prostitution and the Law," *Women, Law, and Social Change*, Shamsuddin Shams, ed. (New Delhi: Ashish Publishing House, 1991) pp.189-194.

[12]Interview with officer, Women-in-Distress Cell, Criminal Investigation Department (CID), Vigilance Branch, Crawford Market Headquarters, August 1994.

violated and "spoiled" and therefore social pariahs; they believed they would never be free to leave for reasons of crushing "debt" to their madams or because they feared violent reprisals; they had nothing to return to; they feared the contempt and rejection of family members; they had no resources, either to make a new life for themselves or to placate their families. Because these women told the police that they did not want to return home, the officers apparently made no effort to free them from the brothel or investigate conditions there or charges of abuse. The police appeared oblivious to the fact that the brothel owners were in violation of the law and that the debt bondage the women described was itself illegal.

One of the women we interviewed, "Santhi," said police raids had been frequent in the brothels where she worked from 1980 to 1991, and when there was a raid the women would hide their customers. There was a special false ceiling where they could hide people. Santhi was arrested once when one night some Bangladeshi police came to the brothel in civilian dress and found a Bangladeshi girl working there who had been sold by her husband to the brothel. All the women in the brothel were rounded up and held in police custody for about three hours. They were not given anything to eat or drink and because the police station was in the middle of town everyone was looking in at them. After some time the brothel owner came, paid the police some money and got them out. The woman from Bangladesh was returned to her village, and everyone else was returned to the brothel. The policemen demanded that the brothel owner pay money to send the Bangladeshi girl back home.

Activists who work with women in prostitution, as well as the brothel inmates interviewed by Human Rights Watch/Asia charged that local policemen regularly took advantage of their power to frequent the kothas as customers. In Calcutta's Sonegachi red-light area, a 1993 study by two epidemiologists with the All India Institute of Hygiene and Public Health found two policemen among every one hundred clients.[13] Testimony from women interviewed by Human Rights Watch/Asia supports their findings.

THE ROLE OF THE NEPALI POLICE

The Nepali police are also complicit in the trafficking of Nepali girls and women to Indian brothels. Villagers and officials in Nuwakot District told Human Rights Watch/Asia that traffickers routinely pay protection money to local police

---

[13]*Telegraph*, "Study Reveals Sonagachi Clientele" (Calcutta, India), October 16, 1993.

and Nepali politicians as "a sort of commission" to prevent arrests and prosecutions. "If a trafficker ends up in prison it means he or she hasn't paid off the police," one villager observed. A journalist who has researched trafficking patterns in Nepal told Human Rights Watch/Asia:

> [E]very point of the border, the police come if they suspect trafficking. But they don't try to arrest, they just take bribes. You can see them go down through the bus collecting money. It's very visible."[14]

Activists and police have confirmed that there is a link between international trafficking and local prostitution in Nepal, and that both industries are on the rise, particularly in urban areas, border towns, and villages along the main east-west highway. In the same towns where reports of trafficking to India are on the increase -- Kathmandu, Birganj, Biratnagar, Nepalgunj -- local prostitution also appears to be growing, with the complicity of local police and officials, according to local activists.

> At the lower levels police are common and frequent customers who take their pleasure free of charge -- and often violently -- as compensation for their "protection." At the higher levels, activists say, an alarming number of ex-Panchayat government officials were involved in both trafficking and local prostitution, and border police still play a major role. Trafficking of girls, especially to India where the demand for young Nepalese increases every day, is probably one of the country's most lucrative "black" industries.[15]

An officer in Birganj told Human Rights Watch/Asia that prostitution was increasing in the town's local guesthouses and wine shops, and also that women who used to be involved only in local prostitution were now also being trafficked to India. The same has been reported of girls from the Badibadini community in the

---

[14]Anonymous interview, Kathmandu, Nepal, March 1994.

[15]Shanti Choudhary, Creative Development Centre, "Every Young Girl's Nightmare," from a 1993 CDC progress report for funding agencies.

western town of Nepalgunj -- "traditional" prostitutes who are now recruited for Indian brothels.[16]

Human rights organizations in Nepal also report consistent complaints of corruption and abuse by police attached to the Hanuman Dhoka district police headquarters in Kathmandu. Most complaints involve torture and mistreatment in detention, arbitrary and unacknowledged arrests, and extortion. In the case described below, which was widely reported in the Nepali press, Thilu Ghale, a woman arrested by police from the Hanuman Dhoka police station in Kathmandu, accused police of torture and of attempted rape and extortion. She reported that in an attempt to secure a large bribe, the police at Hanuman Dhoka police station threatened to sell her to a brothel in India.[17]

The Case of Thilu Ghale[18]

According to a complaint lodged by Thilu Ghale, age twenty-six, a resident of Lazimpat and the owner of a carpet factory, she was arrested while shopping on September 22, 1994, by a group of five or six police officers and taken to Hanuman Dhoka police station in Kathmandu where she was beaten and tortured with electric shocks. In her written complaint, she charged that the police officers also attempted to extort money from her. Press accounts reported that a police officer threatened to sell her to a brothel in India if she did not pay him Rs. 1,300,000 [$26,000]. Soon after her arrest, Ghale was allowed to telephone her mother, but despite two visits to the police station, her mother was not allowed to see her. Thilu Ghale's mother filed a *habeas corpus* petition with the Supreme Court on September 26. On September 28, the court ordered a written response from the police within twenty-four hours.

In a written reply to the court, delivered on September 30, the Kathmandu police denied having arrested Ghale. Ghale was then transferred to the office of the Bhaktapur deputy superintendent of police, about fifteen kilometers from

---

[16]The Badini were originally court dancers and musicians. Many Badini eventually took up prostitution.

[17]"Do Nepali Police Traffic Girls?" *Jan Swatantrata* (Kathmandu, Nepal), October 14, 1993.

[18]See also, "Nepal; Human rights safeguards," Amnesty Insternational, June 1994, ASA 31/02/94, (London: Amnesty International, June 1994) pp. 9-10, and Informal Sector Service Centre (INSEC), *Human Rights Yearbook, 1993,* (Kathmandu: INSEC, April 1994), pp. 46-47.

Kathmandu. According to Ghale's complaint, she was further mistreated at the Bhaktapur station and was denied food for two days. She was, however, able to get a message to her mother. On October 3, the Supreme Court ordered the deputy inspector of Police for Nepal to locate and produce Ghale within twenty-four hours. On October 5, Ghale was produced before the court by the police, who claimed she had been arrested on October 3 and charged before the district court with selling one gram of heroin. A detention order dated October 3 had been issued by the Kathmandu District Court. The case was heard by the Supreme Court on October 6, and Ghale submitted a written account of her arrest and detention, which included the date of her arrest and her treatment in police custody. The court placed her in judicial custody and ordered an inquiry. While in custody, Thilu Ghale was reportedly visited by a senior Home Ministry official who tried to convince her to drop the *habeas corpus* case.

In November, the Supreme Court found that Ghale had indeed been arrested in September. It ordered her release, pending a hearing in Kathmandu District Court on charges of selling drugs. Superintendent of Police Rewat Bahadur Thapa was charged with contempt for lying to the Supreme Court, but to Human Rights Watch/Asia's knowledge, Ghale's allegations of police mistreatment and attempted extortion were not investigated, and no disciplinary action was taken.

Despite consistent reports by human rights groups and journalists that trafficking occurs in Kathmandu, particularly from its carpet factories, and complaints from trafficking victims that they had been trafficked to India from Kathmandu, when Human Rights Watch/Asia visited the Hanuman Dhoka police station in March 1994 and spoke with Superintendent Thapa, the officer denied that trafficking of women was occurring in Kathmandu. "Girl trafficking is not in Kathmandu district. They are all from Sindhupalchowk and Nuwakot -- most are from Sindhupalchowk. None is happening in Kathmandu." Thapa also rejected charges that brokers for Indian brothels were using Kathmandu's carpet factories for recruitment.

> Brokers are not using carpet factories. Brokers are not trying to use Kathmandu because people know them. Brokers are not able to recruit from within carpet factories because they are connected to old village ladies. We get no news from carpet factories -- there are no reports of this type, of criminal activity.[19]

---

[19]Interview with Superintendent of Police Rewant Bahadur Thapa, March 1994.

Denial of Responsibility

Nepali officers interviewed by Human Rights Watch/Asia acknowledged that although they had received directives from police headquarters "to take [trafficking] seriously," there has been no systematic attempt to train police officers to identify possible culprits. The decision to stop and question a suspected trafficker or, more commonly, a suspected trafficking victim, rests solely with the individual officer on duty, who makes the determination based on his subjective assessment of a suspect's appearance. Based on interviews with many police officers, it was clear that their individual perceptions about who was a likely trafficker varied. One police officer described traffickers as typically "men from the Mongolian communities." Another said "most traffickers are women -- ladies, with good relations in Bombay, who bring girls and sell them." Another said his post arrested mostly young men, and a fourth said he stopped mostly girls. An officer in Butwal explained, "If two people don't look alike we suspect something is wrong. We make an arrest if we suspect somebody..." And at the Briganj customs post, an officer told Human Rights Watch/Asia, "We can't arrest everybody. We look at people on rickshaws -- if they have kids we leave them alone. If they look suspicious, we stop them."

This would have been little reassurance to "Sita," who was twenty and had a small child when she and the toddler were trafficked to India by a man who offered to marry her. As noted above, once Sita arrived in Bombay, her son was taken from her and she never saw him again.

The police in Butwal told Human Rights Watch/Asia they knew the town was a transit point for trafficking, but that it was difficult to apprehend traffickers because they often lied about their relationship to the girls, posing as brothers or husbands, or about the nature of their travel. A police officer at the border disagreed: "If a couple who are arrested claimed to be married, but their stories differ or if the second names are different, we arrest them. If they claim to be married we ask them to bring a letter from their VDC [Village Development Community] to prove it. Then only do we allow them to go. On average we have about fifteen cases a month where people are told to return to their villages or asked to bring letters from their VDC." He said that most people who are asked to bring a letter from home do return with one, but also expressed discomfort about requiring such letters, because of the expense and difficulty it posed for people who had travelled long distances.

In general, girls and women attract the most attention at border posts and bus stands, and police target them for arrest. The police at the Sunauli border said that the great majority of people stopped at the border were suspected trafficking victims, but seldom are the trafficker and trafficked arrested together. All police personnel in the border towns were unanimous in asserting that the reason for arresting the girls was that they had no money and needed help getting home. Local police said they arrested girls to get information about their traffickers.

In most interviews with Nepali police, the officers alleged that the problem was worse in other towns, or that primary responsibility for investigations and arrests was with other branches of the police force. The Sunauli border police told Human Rights Watch/Asia that traffickers were rarely identified or arrested at the border. This was usually done in the village from which the girls were taken. They said girls got arrested more frequently because groups typically split up at the border, and the police can only identify the girls. If a girl could not say where she was going or why, she was arrested and sent back to her home district. They also claimed that the criminal gangs who control trafficking operated in Butwal and Narayanghat, not at their border post. Officers at Birganj likewise alleged that the traffickers did not operate in their jurisdictions.

An officer in Butwal, who had earlier acknowledged that Butwal was a transit point for trafficking, later downplayed the problem, saying it was more severe elsewhere. "Generally the traffickers don't want to stop here now. Now they stop on the other side or they go to other small places along the border." He also denied there was an organized gang operating in Butwal.

The Butwal police told Human Rights Watch/Asia that the majority of people they arrested were victims who were sent home, not traffickers. But since they cannot stop to question everyone, they said they only board a bus when they suspect there may be traffickers inside, and they rarely made arrests. The Butwal police claimed it was the border police who made most arrests. Occasionally, police in Butwal said, they receive a complaint from a family that a daughter has disappeared. These reports are sent on to the border police.

> If someone filed a complaint that someone had disappeared from
> a village, we would send a letter to the border police to look for
> them. There is also an NGO in Bombay and we would send a
> letter to them also.

In the five months the inspector had worked in Butwal, he had never located anyone as a result of sending such a letter.

The U.N. Special Rapporteur on the Sale of Children found similar "burden shifting" on the issue of police responsibility for investigating the sale of children to illegal factories in Nepal and concluded, "This type of obfuscation...does not bode well for law enforcement and child protection..."

Another major problem is that there is no provision in the Nepali civil code to protect women against intimidation by those they accuse of being traffickers-- who are normally allowed out on bail after a short time in detention. Police complain that women are pressured or bribed to drop cases they file against their traffickers. And the cases are difficult to win because it takes years for most women to escape the brothel system, and the trail is very cold. An officer in Butwal claimed never to have been pressured to release anyone held in a trafficking case and said he did not know anyone who had. But he admitted that when a trafficking case went to court, there was a potential for intimidation and harassment of the witness. He told Human Rights Watch/Asia that the length of time it takes to complete an investigation and the pressures on the victim encourage many of them to drop their cases. "Until the case actually goes to court, there is a lot of social pressure on the girl, and [public] interest drops after a while, too. Also the traffickers pay off the girls to drop the cases."

The logistical difficulties of arresting a suspected trafficker are compounded by Nepal's terrain, lack of infrastructure, poor communication technology and inefficient procedures. After a family reports its missing daughter to a local constable, the police must convey the report to the district center to obtain an arrest warrant. In some cases this requires traveling for many hours on footpaths in the mountains. If the suspect is found and an arrest is made, the suspect is brought back to the district headquarters for registration and detention pending investigation. Cases filed by the returned victims are equally difficult to investigate, because often years have passed since the girl left home.

Although local police bear primary responsibility for the apprehension of traffickers, their ability to prevent abuse is circumscribed by senior officers who view them as "dangerously untrained." According to Junior Subinspector Shrestha of the Kharanitar village police in Nuwakot district, although arrests can take place in the village, arrest orders and registration of detainees must occur at the district headquarters in Trisuli, thirteen hours away on foot. The Kharanitar police must travel to Trisuli, report the case and get written authorization before returning to the village to bring anyone in for questioning. Those arrested are then sent back to the district center for registration. Although many suspected traffickers from the area served by the Kharanitar police post have been identified, the police there said they had not apprehended a trafficker in the past two years.

> We arrest girls to get to the traffickers, but this post has not arrested any traffickers. There are warrants that have been outstanding for two years for the arrest of traffickers. We have thirty or thirty-five warrants out for traffickers, but we can't find

them. We haven't seen them. Anyway, once the girls are gone,
it's useless to find the traffickers.

The local police said that they detained women who had returned from
India for questioning.

The girls have a right to go to India, but we have a right to
question them. Trafficking is an offense against the state, and we
have orders to question suspected victims. A letter comes from
the district office ordering the questioning of a girl returning ...
Sometimes parents register a case of a girl disappearing, and if
she's found we need to question her. Or somebody from the
village reports it to the police, the police report it to the central
district and the central district gives written authorization for
questioning.

Police and other government officials at the national level defended these
procedures by pointing out that the local police were "uneducated" and ill-trained
and would be likely to abuse detainees if they were not required to report to the
district center before and after arrest.

IMPUNITY FOR TRAFFICKERS AND BROTHEL OWNERS

Senior police officials interviewed by Human Rights Watch/Asia
acknowledged that there is political pressure, or perceived political pressure, to be
lenient with accused traffickers, such as when a parliamentarian called a district
officer to get information on a particular case. They argued, however that it was not
an institutional problem, but one individual's weakness of character and that it was
up to the individual officers to resist such pressure.

But A.R. Panday, chief district officer for Nuwakot District, told Human
Rights Watch/Asia that trafficking cases were notoriously difficult to prove, and
that traffickers frequently used political influence and bribes to avoid prosecution.
Complicit parents avoid arrest by reporting their daughter missing to the police
after enough time has passed to ensure that she and her trafficker have already

crossed the border into India. Local police also come under pressure from criminal gangs involved in trafficking.[20]

According to Panday, the chief district officer is a civil servant, not a member of the police force. He is the highest level government servant in a district. The chief district officer is responsible for law and order but does not have prosecutorial powers. His office can support investigations, but the prosecution and police work is the responsibility of the deputy superintendent of police and the government prosecutor. In a typical trafficking case, a women who has returned from Bombay with the help of the Indian police or an Indian social service organization lodges a complaint against her trafficker with the police in her district. The chief district officer orders a police investigation. If the complaint is deemed credible, a case is filed in the district court by a government prosecutor.

An assistant superintendent of police in Birganj told Human Rights Watch/Asia that the Birganj police station did not keep records on the trafficking arrests they made; the records were sent on to the district of origin where the case is lodged with the district court.

A CWIN newspaper survey between April and September 1992 found that 35 percent of all reported cases of sexual offenses implicated police or politicians. Regarding trafficking, CWIN reported:

> Accusations of state corruption and complicity in the trade are fueled by ministers and politicians frequently ordering the release of offenders held by the police in Sindhupalchowk, Nuwakot and Makwanpur districts. Whereas reports of rape or abduction are frequent, those recording punishment of offenders are rare.[21]

---

[20]State officials did acknowledge that pressure on local police from criminal gangs operating within communities could be intense, and argued that programs to promote awareness in communities where trafficking occurs could help combat it. Local police, who are far more vulnerable to reprisals by these gangs, and more likely to benefit from the good-will of powerful local bosses, denied any knowledge of criminal gangs operating in areas under their jurisdiction.

[21]Informal Sector Service Centre (INSEC), *Human Rights Yearbook, 1992,* (Kathmandu: INSEC, April 1993), see also, Child Workers in Nepal, *Voice of Child Workers,* "Road to Bombay," Issue No 15/16 (Kathmandu: CWIN, December 1992), p.48.

Political parties reportedly play an important role in trafficking in Nuwakot district where traffickers were said to make campaign contributions in return for protection. The chief district officer for Nuwakot explained that Nuwakot district was especially complicated because there were three MPs from three different parties represented -- Nepali Congress, Communist Party and the Rastriya Prajatantra Party -- each with its own constituency.

> When someone does a crime he tries to buy protection from politicians, MPs. The MPs are silent on this [trafficking] issue. There is no political or social commitment, they are most interested in getting votes from their voters... Kansa Lama, he was a trafficker who was arrested, was protected by politicians, bailed himself out and escaped.[22]

The arrest of Ranjeet Lama in June 1993 and Simla Tamang in September 1993 brought into unprecedented public focus the role of Nepali officials in the trafficking industry and the influence wielded by wealthy brothel owners. Simla Tamang, who was convicted of trafficking in January 1994 , admitted in court to owning some 500 prostitutes in Bombay. Ranjeet Lama, her nephew, admitted to trafficking girls to brothels in Bombay owned by his wife Sita, who reportedly owned nearly 400 girls and women.

Both Ranjeet and Simla have been linked to public officials, who were reported to have intervened on their behalf after they were arrested. The chief district officer of Sindhupalchowk, Dhruba Wagley, complained to the press in September 1993 that a Rastriya Prajatantra Party (RPP) member of parliament and former cabinet minister, Pasupati Shamsher Rana, and other local leaders were pressuring him to release Ranjeet from custody. Wagley told a journalist with the *Kantipur Daily* that Ranjeet had contributed five million rupees to Pasupati Shamsher's last campaign.

According to local journalists, Simla was in her own right an important public figure, who reportedly threatened to run against Pasupati Shamsher Rana in the 1981 Rastriya Panchayat election. In 1986, journalists report that she donated one million rupees to then Prime Minister Marich Man Singh for earthquake relief. She has reportedly donated large amounts of money for the construction of schools

---

[22]Interview with chief district officer A.R. Panday, Nuwakot District, March 2, 1995.

and temples in Sindhupalchowk district. Simla Tamang's husband is reported to be a member of the Nuwakot District Development Committee.[23]

Simla grew up in Mahankal, Sindhupalchowk, where her parents still live. Soon after her arrest, Simla Tamang accused her uncle, Gyan Bahadur Tamang, of selling her to a brothel twenty-five years before.

According to the *Kathmandu Post*, on September 13, 1993, just days after the arrest of Simla Tamang, Kamala Lama, the wife of Dawa Phintso, a former Rastriya Panchayat member from Rasuwa District, was also arrested in Kathmandu on trafficking charges. Arrested along with her were four others, Dhan Bahadur, Jama Bahadur, Lila Tamang and Asha Tamang.[24]

> Research and surveys on the trafficking of women have revealed that there is a close link between police and politics where prostitution is concerned....Quite often the local administration or police of Sindhupalchok, Makawanpur and Nuwakot districts have released accused persons due to the direct command of ministries and politicians. In the same light, a photo album consisting of 125 young women was found during a police raid of Mr. D.B. Lama's home. Mr. D.B. Lama, the former Inspector General of Police (IGP), was arrested in connection with the trafficking of women. Fortunately, newspapers often disclose facts about police involvement in protecting criminals and in sexual violence such as rape and abduction. Unfortunately, the criminals are rarely punished.[25]

The home of former IGP D.B. Lama was raided in 1987. He was arrested, and the Royal Army took over investigation of his case. No further information regarding the charges against him or the sentence served is available.

---

[23]*Kantipur Daily*, "Arrest of a Flesh Trade Crime Gang; Turmoil in the Crime World," Bhadra 21, 2050 (September 1993).

[24]*Kathmandu Post*, September 17, 1993.

[25] Child Workers in Nepal, Concerned Centre(CWIN),"The Road to Bombay," *Voice of Child Workers*, Issue 15 & 16 (Kathmandu, Nepal), December 1992, p. 48.

THE DANGERS OF DISSENT

The trafficking network is vast, reaching from India's largest cities to Nepal's most remote villages, yet the brothel owners and managers in Bombay, the brokers, the agents and the victims are frequently from the same villages and communities. Local residents in Nepal's hill villages who oppose trafficking said they were afraid of the criminal gangs that operate in their areas. The few individuals who were outspoken in their opposition complained that they were shunned and harassed by their neighbors.

Villagers in Dupche, Nuwakot, told researchers with the human rights organization INSEC (Informal Sector Service Centre) in early 1993 that influential people from the area were running brothels in India and that "gallas" (centers from where girls are recruited) had been set up in the village itself. They charged that two daughters of a village leader were working in Bombay at the time, as was the niece of a national-level politician from the area.[26] These charges were repeated frequently by Nuwakot residents and others in Nepal when Human Rights Watch/Asia visited in 1994.

One Nuwakot resident told Human Rights Watch/Asia that almost every household in his village had daughters in India, and some had three or four. In 1993 he said he had tried to start an educational campaign against trafficking, but his neighbors got angry. He gave up when he found he could not interest local police or politicians in the project. He believes the trafficking network in Nuwakot operates with police complicity.

> People who protest trafficking are in the minority. It is very difficult to fight because everyone is unified -- all are involved in trafficking in one way or another. The families are profiting, so no one will talk.
>
> There is such a big gang nobody can do anything. They have so many agents. This is very high level. The gang uses adult women from the village itself who know the police. If a girl goes through the gang they will guarantee safe passage all the way to the border. They use a lot of people. Only families who try to sell on their own get arrested. Even if the police do arrest

---

[26]Informal Sector Service Centre (INSEC), *Women's Initiation to Fight Against Women's Victimization; A Reports of Victim Women's Forum*, (Nepalgunj: INSEC, February 1993), P.46.

someone, they just take their money and release them. But through the gang there is no problem at all. Only individuals get arrested.

This man told Human Rights Watch/Asia that although he had been criticized by his neighbors for his outspokenness, and that a man who owed him money had refused to pay him, so far nothing more serious had happened.

In Sindhupalchowk, advocacy against trafficking has proven more dangerous. According to CWIN, in Mahankal,

> Villagers hate individuals, government agencies and nongovernmental organisations that campaign for the abolition of prostitution and girl trafficking. These villagers take the individuals and social organisations as their enemies who are trying to deprive them of a livelihood. They, in connivance with the agents, are reported to have made attempts on the lives of some social workers working for the abolition of trafficking and have often warned them not to create any obstacles to their activities.[27]

CWIN noted that trafficking agents had told villagers not to cooperate with outsiders asking questions about trafficking, and that the organization's researchers had found "a couple of villagers... advising other villagers not to talk to social workers, law enforcement personnel or journalists."[28]

This antagonism reached a peak after a major trafficking ring that recruited in the village was exposed in 1993 with the arrest of Simla Tamang, the infamous brothel owner mentioned above. After the arrests began in June 1993, traffickers with ties to rival political parties apparently engaged in a campaign to expose their competitors. Shortly after her arrest Simla [who is said to have links to both the Rastriya Prajatantra Party and the Nepali Congress] accused her uncle, Jyam Bahadur, of having arranged her own trafficking years before. Jyam Bahadur was subsequently arrested, reportedly on the basis of information provided by Juthe Tamang, another Sindhupalchowk resident suspected of ties to the trafficking industry. Juthe Tamang, whose arrest was ordered by Sindhupalchowk's chief

---

[27]Child Workers in Nepal, (CWIN), "The Road to Bombay," *Voice of Child Workers* (Kathmandu) Issue 15 & 16, December 1992, p.52.

[28]Ibid.

district officer in September, was reportedly affiliated with the Communist Party of Nepal-Unified Marxist Leninist (CPN-UML) as was the deputy superintendent of police for Sindhupalchowk, Krishna Kumar Tamang. Juthe Tamang disappeared in January 1994. The human rights organization INSEC reported that two other residents of Sindhupalchowk suspected of involvement in the trafficking industry, Sonam Lama and Purna Tamang, may be responsible for his disappearance because he exposed their activities. The two were said to be affiliated with the Nepali Congress Party and had evaded arrest.[29]

HEALTH CARE, BIRTH CONTROL AND AIDS

The first AIDS cases in Nepal were discovered in 1986 among Western tourists and Nepali women who had returned from Indian brothels. By February 1994, Nepal's Ministry of Health had recorded 199 confirmed cases of HIV infection in Nepal; the figure has continued to climb. The majority of those who have tested positive for HIV in Nepal do not know they carry the virus because they were tested anonymously by Nepal's Ministry of Health as part of a survey it conducted for statistical purposes. The World Health Organization (WHO) estimates that there are over 5,000 people infected with HIV in Nepal and that by the end of the twentieth century, the infection rate in Nepal will reach 100,000.[30] Low literacy rates in Nepal's villages contribute to misinformation and ignorance about HIV-related illness and death. Nepali men who go abroad for work have also contributed to the spread of the disease within their communities. Many of these men, who come to India to work as domestic servants, laborers and watchmen, visit brothels in India and carry the disease back to their home villages in Nepal. Nepali health workers estimate that 300,000 migrant laborers cross the border annually for seasonal work in Indian urban centers, and many will bring back the "Bombay disease" on reentry into Nepal.[31]

A government health official in Nepal, interviewed in March 1994, told Human Rights Watch/Asia:

---

[29]INSEC, *Human Rights Yearbook, 1992,* (Kathmandu: INSEC, 1993) p. 209.

[30]*India Today* article by Ramesh Menon reprinted in Nexus, Population Services International, Delhi, April 1, 1994.

[31]*Illustrated Weekly of India* (Bombay), July 17-23, 1993.

Women who are HIV positive are thrown out of the Indian brothels. The Indian police hand them over to the Nepali police. I haven't heard of cases of girls being turned away at the Nepal border, but it's possible. It may be the police aren't well trained, aren't informed of the policy and don't want to deal with them. The government's policy is to accept them.

During a girl's time in [police] detention, if she is sick and a doctor strongly suspects HIV, the doctor very likely will test her. The ministry recommends consent. It is the official policy that the doctor should get her consent before testing for HIV, but often the doctor just says, "I want to do this test" and doesn't explain, and the girl doesn't know to refuse. We are trying to discourage this.

In Kathmandu there are six hospitals that do blood screening. The ministry has tested a total of 150,000 samples since they began testing. They have found 199 positive cases; there have been twenty-sex cases of full-blown AIDS and thirteen have died. There is no AZT or other drug available for treatment although India may soon begin producing AZT at a price that may make it affordable. There is no access to the drug at present, and as a matter of policy we are not giving the drug.[32]

In India, WHO estimates that as many as 1.5 million people in India may be infected with the HIV virus, with the state of Maharashtra leading the nation in HIV infections.[33] The Indian Council of Medical Research, which estimates that there are a total of about one million commercial sex workers in India, predicts that there will be around 2.5 million sexually transmitted HIV infections in India by the year 2000.

Clinical surveys done by the Indian Health Organisation (IHO) find that 80 percent of sex workers are infected with a sexually transmitted disease (STD),

---

[32]Interview with Dr. B. K. Suvedi, Senior Medical Officer, Ministry of Health, Department of Health Services National AIDS Control Centre. Teku, Kathmandu, Nepal, March 1994.

[33]*Reuters News Service*, "India: Drug Users Spread AIDS in Northeast Indian State," February 25, 1995.

with 50 percent having two or more STDs concomitantly. The most common STDs seen are syphilis, chancroid, gonorrhea, Donovanosis, and venereal warts. Instances of herpes genitalis are on the increase. A newspaper report quoted Maharashtra state officials as estimating that 50 percent of the sex workers in Bombay are infected with HIV. Dr. I.S. Gilada of the IHO has an even higher estimate of over 60 percent infected, a dramatic increase from the finding of 0.6 percent in the IHO's first Bombay red-light study in 1986. The organization's studies show that red-light districts in other metropolitan cities have an HIV infection rate ranging from 30 percent to 50 percent. The same press source quotes one young infected Nepali girl in prostitution, who was lured from her home with the promise of a job and subsequently sold to a brothel in Bombay, as saying: "I am not living even now. So, how does it matter if I die." [34]

Awareness of AIDS among potential customers has driven the sex industry to supply more and more young girls, who can be sold as virgins and therefore AIDS-free. By the same token, the turnover rate among those working as prostitutes is also likely to accelerate as more customers demand "clean" girls, particularly virgins.

> Because many of the girls now contract AIDS sooner or later, there is a growing demand for "fresh meat" that the traditional villages cannot meet, and traffickers have begun looking for Nepali girls of all castes and localities. Girls who test positive for AIDS are immediately dismissed and, visibly sick and without money, are either ostracized by their families or unwilling to go home. Some of them stay in India to die, while many of them come home to work in the streets and brothels of Kathmandu and other Nepalese cities.[35]

The Nepalis are powerless to negotiate any terms of sex in order to protect themselves from HIV infection. They have virtually no say over whether or not to "service" a particular customer, how many customers to accept in a given day, condom use or the type of sex, much less payment. Young girls, some only thirteen or fourteen years old, may be particularly at risk. Not only are they often too intimidated even to attempt to negotiate the terms of sex, but preliminary medical research suggests that the younger the girl, the more susceptible she may be to HIV

---

[34]"Squalor, Disease in City Brothels," *Times of India* (Bombay), August 8, 1994, p.5

[35]Shanti Chaudary, "Every Young Girl's Nightmare," Creative Development Centre.

infection for physiological reasons.[36] Nepali women and girls who attempt to refuse customers often face retaliation. The owners and pimps threaten them with physical harm, beat them, or allow the customers to do so.

People who worked with returnees in Nepal said that there was HIV testing in some Bombay brothels, and that some brothels did appear to discard girls who tested positive. But girls are not always told of their status. There have been only four recorded cases in Nuwakot district of returnees testing positive for HIV, but people in Nuwakot have very little knowledge about the transmission of the virus, and girls who are infected with sexually transmitted diseases remain hesitant to contact physicians. Activists there have also encountered cases of forced sterilization of brothel inmates, hysterectomies during abortion being the most typical.

What emerges from the girls' testimonies is a pattern of transmission from male customers to young girls that calls into question the common perception that prostitutes are the "source" of HIV/AIDS. To be sure, once infected, the Nepali girls in the brothels are likely to infect their customers. But whereas their clients can choose to use condoms or to abstain from sex, the women and girls have no such choice; they are captive partners.

Access to Information about HIV/AIDS

The Indian government has thus far failed to summon the necessary political will and financial resources to inform and educate Nepali women and girls in brothels. Brothel operators are allowed to dictate the terms of access for health educators, and to limit visits to clinics. The language barrier is also a major obstacle: most Nepali women and girls do not speak or read sufficient Hindi or Marathi to communicate in all but the simplest of terms with non-Nepali speakers; many are illiterate. To our knowledge there are no official educational materials in the Nepali language, whether written pamphlets or public service announcements for television or radio, the latter two being the most common sources of information for our interviewees. In our interviews, Human Rights Watch/Asia learned that only a small percentage of the Nepali women and girls who had

---

[36]Because the mucous membrane of the genital tract in girls is not as thick as that of a grown women, medical researchers have hypothesized that it is a less efficient barrier to viruses. Moreover, young women may be less efficient than older women in producing mucous, which has an immune function. United Nations Development Programme, "Young Women: Silence, Susceptibility and the HIV Epidemic."

worked in brothels in India had any knowledge about the transmission of HIV/AIDS.

- "Sita" said she had heard about AIDS, but only that it was a dangerous disease. She thought you only got infected by blood, but she wasn't sure what kind of blood was meant.

- "Devi" said condoms were not available in any of the brothels in which she worked and that the girls did not seem to know anything about AIDS. She thought if they really knew about the dangers of AIDS they would have tried to run away. Devi had only heard about AIDS on the radio since she returned to Nepal, but did not understand much about it. She thought it might be transmitted if you ate the food of someone with the disease. She said that in the brothels, old prostitutes used to give the younger girls their leftovers because they got more to eat, but Devi did not like to eat their food. She had not been to a doctor since she got back, but she is not afraid of diseases. She feels fine.

- "Maya" never asked clients to use condoms because she did not know they could prevent AIDS. She said she had heard about AIDS but did not know anything about it. Because she stayed in the brothel only a short time, she did not know the symptoms.

- "Santhi" said when she began working in the brothels condoms were not available, but after three or four years, girls began buying them themselves and would offer them to the customers. They knew nothing about AIDS, but "if customers used them we felt clean." The girls in the brothels where Santhi worked also tried to make a profit on condoms, buying them for 25 p. [less than a cent] a piece and selling them for two rupees. Most customers refused to use them.

- After "Neela" was arrested in a raid on the brothel where she worked, she was placed in a shelter for children and her blood was tested for HIV. She was told the doctors wanted a blood sample because she might have a contagious disease, but they never told her what disease they were testing for. Afterwards she was told by the shelter staff that she had tested positive for HIV and that all the other girls had tested negative. Neela said she knew little about HIV before she returned to Nepal, but that in the brothel one girl was supposed to have been HIV positive and the manager told the girls not to eat her food.

Brothel owners and managers paint a rosier picture of AIDS awareness in Bombay, and one of the ways health organizations in Bombay attempt to convince local brothel owners to use condoms is to appeal to their desire to turn a profit. Women exposed to these programs know the dangers of AIDS and claim to use condoms, but in practice, customers frequently refuse them.

A gharwali in Bombay, who was also a client of a local AIDS awareness program, told Human Rights Watch/Asia that she thought AIDS was one of the reasons for a troubling decrease in business.

Customers are falling off in great numbers. Three to five a day is a large number these days. But somehow, for some reason, they also still keep coming. Those men who want to live stay away. Young unmarried men who don't care that much, don't worry that much about living, or responsibilities to wife and kids, they keep on coming.

V. THE APPLICABLE LAW

There is no shortage of applicable law addressing trafficking in women and other abuses typical of the brothel industry. Both international and domestic laws prohibit slavery and all similar practices, including the sale of persons, forced labor and debt bondage. There are also specific prohibitions against the trafficking of adults and children for prostitution and other forms of sexual exploitation. Among those fundamental human rights guaranteed by international law but frequently denied trafficking victims are state protection against arbitrary detention, torture, including sexual assault and rape, and other cruel, inhuman or degrading treatment. International law obligates the state to protect individuals against such abuse, even when it is committed by a private actor. Such crimes are also prohibited under Indian and Nepali law. The problem lies in enforcement, which is rare and inconsistent, and in the active perpetuation of trafficking-related abuse by corrupt and complicit officials.

INTERNATIONAL LAW

India is a signatory to most international human rights instruments relevant to trafficking in women and girls, including the Convention for the Suppression of Traffic in Persons and of the Exploitation of the Prostitution of Others (The Trafficking Convention), the International Covenant on Civil and Political Rights (ICCPR), and antislavery conventions. While Nepal has not ratified the Trafficking Convention, it is a party to the ICCPR and to the Supplementary Convention on the Abolition of Slavery, the Slave Trade and Institutions and Practices Similar to Slavery (1956). Both governments have ratified the Convention on the Elimination of All Forms of Discrimination Against Women (CEDAW) and the Convention on the Rights of the Child (CRC), which obligate states parties to ensure protection against discrimination and to take all appropriate measures to suppress all forms of trafficking in women and children.

Articles 34 and 35 of the Convention on the Rights of the Child direct states parties to "take all appropriate national, bilateral and multinational measures to prevent the abduction, sale or traffic of children for any purpose or in any form" and specifically charge signatories with the protection of children from sexual exploitation and abuse.[1]

While CEDAW does not set forth specific measures with regard to the suppression of trafficking of women, earlier conventions do. The 1949 trafficking convention calls on states parties to punish traffickers and to protect all persons against such abuse.[2] As a signatory to this convention, India has a clear obligation under international law to take action against traffickers and protect victims from the abuses documented in this report. India is also a party to ICCPR and is thus obligated to ensure that persons are not subjected to arbitrary detention and torture or cruel, inhuman or degrading treatment or punishment.[3]

---

[1]Article 19, CRC. Article 19 of the Convention directs states parties to take legislative and judicial measures to protect children from "all forms of physical or mental violence, injury or abuse...maltreatment or exploitation, including sexual abuse... ." Article 11 of the CRC also calls on states parties to "take measures to combat the illicit transfer and non-return of children abroad" and to undertake bilateral and multilateral agreements to do so. Article 37 of the Convention also includes safeguards against torture, mistreatment, arbitrary arrest and detention.

[2]The Convention for the Suppression of the Traffic in Persons and the Exploitation of the Prostitution of Others was approved by the United Nations General Assembly in 1949. Article 1 calls on states parties to punish any person who: "(1) Procures, entices or leads away, for the purposes of prostitution, another person, even with the consent of that person;(2) Exploits the prostitution of another person, even with the consent of that person." Article 2 calls for the punishment of any person who "keeps or manages, or knowingly finances or takes part in the financing of a brothel." It also obligates states to punish those who knowingly rent out property for the purpose of prostitution. Article 17 obligates states to adopt measures to check trafficking in persons. The Convention also calls on states parties "so far as possible" to "make suitable provisions for [trafficking victims'] temporary care and maintenance;" to repatriate persons "only after agreement...with the State of destination," and, where persons cannot pay the cost of repatriation, to bear the cost "as far as the nearest frontier."Convention for the Suppression of the Traffic in Persons, Article 19.

[3]Article 7 of the ICCPR prohibits torture and other forms of "cruel, inhuman or degrading treatment or punishment." Article 8 contains prohibitions against slavery, servitude and forced labor. Article 9 protects against arbitrary arrest and guarantees the right to liberty and security of person. Article 2 of the ICCPR obligates states to ensure the protection of these rights regardless of whether the violation has been committed by

Forced labor and slavery are prohibited by Article 8 of the International Covenant on Civil and Political Rights and Article 4 of the Universal Declaration of Human Rights. In addition, the International Labor Organization passed the Forced Labor Convention (No. 29) in 1930, to which India is a party. This convention calls on its signatories to "suppress the use of forced or compulsory labour in all its forms in the shortest period possible."[4] At its 40th session in 1957, the ILO further clarified its definition of forced labor to specifically incorporate debt-bondage and serfdom[5] and it passed the Abolition of Forced Labour Convention (No. 105). India has not ratified ILO Convention No.105.

INDIA'S LAWS

Trafficking in human beings and the abuses associated with it are also explicitly prohibited under a wide range of India's domestic laws, including the Indian constitution, specific anti-trafficking acts, the Indian penal code, and in state and local ordinances.

The Indian constitution specifically prohibits trafficking in persons. Article 23, in the fundamental rights section of the constitution, states, "traffic in human beings...and other similar forms of forced labour are prohibited." Article 39 guarantees equal treatment of men and women and obligates the state to ensure "that the health and strength of workers, men and women...and children are not abused...and that children and youth are protected against exploitation..." Article 42 provides protection against inhumane working conditions.

The two principal laws that address trafficking and prostitution are the Suppression of Immoral Traffic in Women and Girls Act of 1956 (SITA), and the Immoral Traffic in Persons Prevention Act of 1986 (ITPPA), colloquially called PITA, an amendment to SITA. Neither law prohibits prostitution *per se*, but both

---

state forces or by private parties.

[4]The Forced Labour Convention (No. 29) defines "forced or compulsory labour" as "all work or service which is extracted from a person under the menace of any penalty and for which the said person has not offered himself voluntarily."

[5]ILO, *Conventions and Recommendations 1919-1966*, Adopted by the ILO, (Geneva: ILO, 1966), p. 891.

target commercialized vice and forbid soliciting.[6] SITA's chief drawback was its criminalization of the female practitioner of prostitution. The language of the law defined the prostitute as female, thereby exempting males in prostitution from criminalization. Even the sentencing procedures discriminated against the woman: a woman arrested for soliciting under SITA could be imprisoned for up to a year, but a pimp for only three months.[7] SITA allowed prosecution of persons other than the women only if the persons involved "knowingly" or "willingly" made women prostitute themselves. Accordingly, pimps, brothel owners, madams, and procurers could feign ignorance of prostitution and escape punishment. Similarly, the client was not viewed as an offender and could not be penalized under SITA.[8] In addition, SITA only addressed street prostitution; prostitution behind closed doors was left alone -- a condition that actually promoted the establishment of brothels.

---

[6]SITA, a penal law, was passed in 1956 and enforced in 1958 as a consequence of India's signing the Trafficking Convention, rather than as a result of any mass social welfare movement. SITA did not seek the "abolition of prostitutes and prostitution as such and to make it per se a criminal offense or punish a person because one prostitutes oneself." Its stated goal was "to inhibit or abolish commercialised vice, namely the traffic in persons for the purpose of prostitution as an organised means of living." Prostitution was defined as the act of a female who offers her body for promiscuous sexual intercourse for hire. Accordingly, the engagement by a woman in individual, voluntary, and independent prostitution was not an offense.

[7]The law permitted penalization of a woman found to be engaged in prostitution under certain conditions. For example, Section 7(i) penalized a woman found engaged in prostitution in or near a public place. Section 8(b) did the same for a woman found seducing or soliciting for purposes of prostitution. The law also permitted a magistrate to order the removal of a person engaged in prostitution from any place, and to punish the person upon refusal. Offenses under SITA were bailable, but a woman picked up from the street by the police usually did not have either the money or the influence to keep herself out of custody or free from fines.

[8]Indeed, clients sometimes were called as witnesses against women accused of prostitution. Police could arrest clients only by applying the indecent behavior and obscenity sections available under local laws, or the Indian Penal Code. For example, Section 110B of the Bombay Police Act penalizes indecent behavior and allows for the arrest of pimps and prostitutes.

The Immoral Traffic in Persons Prevention Act of 1986 (ITPPA),[9] amended the 1956 SITA in important ways. However, its basic goals and premises remain much the same as those of SITA. Although prostitution as such is not prohibited under ITPPA, ITPPA contains nine punishable conditions, including brothel keeping, abetting in brothel keeping, living off brothel earnings, procuring, detaining, activity in vicinity of public places, seducing or soliciting.[10] By implication, ITPPA recognizes that men and children can also be sexually exploited for commercial purposes. ITPPA includes new categories of offenses and punishments, making it easier to prosecute brothel-keepers and others involved in trafficking. Procurers of prostitutes or those found guilty of inducing someone to undertake prostitution are subject to a prison sentence of three to seven years and a fine of Rs.2000 [$66]; a second conviction carries a mandatory sentence of seven to fourteen years. A first conviction for brothel-keeping under the ITPPA carries a mandatory prison term of one to three years of rigorous imprisonment and a fine of Rs.2000 [$66]. A second conviction is punishable by two to five years of rigorous imprisonment and a fine of Rs.2000. A person convicted of living on the earnings of a prostitute is subject to seven years of imprisonment and a fine of

---

[9]The changes in the title of the Act represented important conceptual as well as policy shifts, most importantly, the recognition of the range of victims was extended from women and girls to persons. Various other definitions were reworked in the 1986 Act. Prostitution, which had been "the act of a female offering her body for promiscuous sexual intercourse for hire," became "the sexual exploitation or abuse of persons for commercial purposes." The shift in emphasis from promiscuity to exploitation was particularly significant, especially for Nepali women whose abuse was justified on the basis of their reputed "promiscuity."

[10]Under ITPPA a brothel was redefined broadly as any place where sexual exploitation or abuse occurred. Accordingly, under Section 3 of ITPPA, the keepers of any place where sexual abuse occurred could be prosecuted. In the case of trafficked women, this would now cover the houses and room where the newly-trafficked girls and women were physically and psychologically broken, in the process called "training." ITPPA also attempted to eliminate the loophole of lack of knowledge which SITA afforded brothel keepers and owners by placing the burden of proof on the landlord conditionally. However, the primary condition under which ITPPA could presume that a landlord had knowledge of the illegalities on his premises was extremely unlikely to be met and therefore effectively useless: that a newspaper report named his premises as used for prostitution.

Rs.1000[$33] or ten years if the prostitute is a child. Any person who engages in prostitution in a public place and any customer with whom the prostitution is carried out is subject to up to three months of imprisonment. If the offense involves a minor, the prison term can range from seven years to life. However, while the act has expanded the circle of persons subject to prosecution, the woman herself remained among those subject to arrest,[11] and in the case of soliciting, subject to much longer terms of imprisonment than a man found guilty of the same offense.[12]

ITPPA also expanded police power to prevent trafficking, but also recognized the potential abuse of power, such as verbal, physical and sexual harassment, by the police during raids. SITA had empowered a Special Police Officer to conduct a search of any premises without a warrant, but now ITPPA extended these powers to the accompanying trafficking police officers who entered the premises. However, ITPPA prohibited male police officers empowered under the act from making a search unless accompanied by two female police officers. Questioning of women and girls had to be undertaken by female police officers. If this was not possible, the women and girls could be questioned only in the presence of a female member of a recognized welfare organization. The act also mandated rehabilitation in "protective homes," shelters or reformatories where education and

---

[11]In Bombay, women are also subject to prosecution for indecent exposure or soliciting in public places under various legal provisions including ITPA, the Bombay Police Act, and the Indian Penal Code.

[12]Many of the amendments ITPPA made to the 1956 law endeavored to broaden the act to include both men and women, and all parties involved in prostitution. But in some cases the amendments actually served to further discriminate against women in prostitution. For example, according to ITPPA, whoever attempts to solicit "by words, gestures, wilful exposure of her person ...for the purpose of prostitution," shall be subject to up to one year imprisonment (six months for a first offense) and a fine of up to Rs. 500 [$16]. But a 1986 amendment to the law adds that if the offense is committed by a man, the mandatory sentence ranges from only seven days to three months.

living facilities were to be provided.[13] ITPPA did not give police the power to actually close brothels.

Unlike SITA, ITPPA was concerned about prostitution of minors and children, and introduced stiff penal measures against those who profited with punishment of not less than seven years and not more than ten years.[14] ITPPA's additional clause addressing the offense of procuring carried rigorous imprisonment of seven to fourteen years in the case of a minor, and seven years to life in the case of a child. Similarly, prostitution of a minor or child in a public place was punishable with seven years to life, or up to ten years along with a fine. However, these measures were effectively weakened by the discretionary powers given by ITPPA to the court to reduce the term of imprisonment to below the seven

---

[13]However, a Supreme Court review of one such facility in Delhi between 1979 and 1981, and subsequent independent studies conducted in 1990 of the same home and of the Liluah home in Calcutta found that inmates of "protective homes," including former brothel inmates, women charged with criminal offenses and "non-criminal lunatics," were housed together in appalling conditions, denied adequate food and clothing and provided with no vocational training. There were also reports of forced prostitution and bonded labor. In the Liluah Home for Destitute Women, in Calcutta, a survey by university students found the institution to be severely overcrowded. Inmates complained of grave mistreatment including branding with hot irons, rapes and sexual assaults. Almost all inmates were suffering from malnutrition. Many also had chronic skin diseases and tuberculosis. See, *Telegraph*," House of Horror; The Liluah Home: Where inmates are starved, assaulted, degraded, molested and humiliated," (Calcutta) July 29, 1990. See also Arun Bhandari et al., *Women and AIDS: Denial and Blame; A Citizen's Report,* (New Delhi: Saraswati Art Press, ovember-December 1990), pp.46-49.

[14]Girls and women received different treatment under SITA, although their exploiters did not. SITA had defined adulthood as twenty-one years. Accordingly, an adult woman prosecuted for soliciting or prostituting in a public place would be tried in court and, if convicted, sent to a protective home or institution, whereas a girl was immediately referred for rehabilitation. However, the punishments for exploiters of women and girls were the same. Now, ITPPA made distinctions between "major," "minor," and "child." The Act defined as a "child" anyone who was under sixteen years of age. Persons between sixteen and eighteen years were considered "minors," and anyone eighteen or older was an adult or "major." Contrary to the protections of international law, for adults, ITPPA reverses the burden of proof. While children and minors arrested under the act were presumed innocent, those over eighteen were required to prove their innocence.

year minimum for offenses such as detaining a person for prostitution or seduction of a person in custody.[15]

Other existing legislation, including the Bonded Labour System (Abolition) Act and article 376 of the Indian penal code (IPC), explicitly forbids the purchase and sale of human beings, forced labor and all forms of bonded labor. The IPC also prohibits the trafficking and sale of minors.[16] In addition, since many brothel inmates are under eighteen and most report the systematic use of threats and physical assaults to force new girls to serve customers, existing rape, assault, and abduction laws can be used to address the systematic abuse of women and girls in brothels.[17] Article 375 of the IPC defines rape as the act of engaging in sexual

---

[15]The implications of this provisions are particularly serious for women and girls trafficked over long distances, as in the case of Nepali women and girls. Not only does the exercise of the court's discretionary power dilute the general legal threat to persons who traffic women from abroad, but it also reduces the effective impact of laws against other abductors and kidnappers who imprison women and girls in brothels far from their homes. Women and girls transported over long distances and detained for prostitution face greater obstacles in attempting to escape from the brothel system, due to distance, and differences of language and culture. Even if they manage to escape from their original captors they risk falling prey to other abductors and kidnappers who do not fear long jail sentences for their actions. ITPPA introduced another clause whereby if a person was found with a child in a brothel it would be presumed, unless proved to the contrary, that the child had been detained for prostitution.

[16] In addition. Sections 372 and 373 of the IPC state that anyone who buys, sells or obtains possession of any person under the age of eighteen for the purpose of prostitution, illicit intercourse, unlawful or immoral purposes, or knowing that such use at any age is likely, is subject to up to ten years of imprisonment. The IPC also contains prohibitions against indecent assaults on women (Section 354), kidnapping, abduction, and wrongful confinement (Sections 359-368), and mandates imprisonment of up to ten years for the procurement or import of minors for the purposes of illicit intercourse, kidnapping and abduction leading to grievous hurt, slavery or subjection to "unnatural lust" (Section 367).

[17]In the case of sexual assault by police or police complicity in sexual abuse of trafficking victims, the Criminal Law (Amendment) Act of 1983, enacted as a result of a 1983 case of custodial violence against women in police lock-ups in Mathura, provides for the offense of custodial rape and prescribes a mandatory ten years of imprisonment for police officers who rape a woman in custody. Custody is customarily understood to

intercourse with a woman when the act is against her will; without her consent; with her consent, when her consent has been obtained by putting her or any person in whom she is interested in fear of death or injury; with her consent when she is incapable of understanding the consequence of her consent; or when she is under sixteen years of age. Under the IPC a minimum term of seven years of imprisonment may be imposed for rape. Rape laws are applicable to both brothel staff and customers.[18]

A report released in May 1994 by the Ministry of Human Resources Development's (HRD) Central Advisory Committee on Prostitution[19] acknowledged the organized and international nature of the trafficking industry and the use of coercion and force in procuring women and girls for prostitution. The report called for paramilitary forces to check the entry of females from abroad and advocated implementation of Section 13(4) of the ITPPA which authorizes the appointment of a centralized anti-trafficking force with interstate jurisdiction. In June 1994, the Central Bureau of Investigation (CBI) responded to the HRD Ministry's invitation and agreed to assume responsibility for trafficking enforcement, pending additional funding.[20]

The state of Maharashtra, of which Bombay is the capital, also addressed trafficking of women in its *Policy for Women*, announced in June 1994.[21] The document highlighted the particular vulnerability of women who had been sold into prostitution and targeted funding for a wide range of programs of police

---

include situations where the victim is effectively under the control of the police or security forces and is not limited to conditions of detention in a prison or lock-up.

[18]Male brothel staff who use rape to "break in" new girls are clearly subject to these laws. In addition, section 376 of the IPC states: "Where a woman is raped by one or more in a group of persons acting in furtherance of their common intention, each of the persons shall be deemed to have committed gang rape within the meaning of this subsection."

[19]Part of the Human Resources Ministry's Department of Women and Child Development.

[20]*The Pioneer* (Delhi, India) June 28, 1994.

[21]Section eight also proposes measures to address unequal and unhappy marriages, domestic violence, and the establishment of legal aid facilities.

reorganization and training designed to address women's protection and safety. The Maharashtra government, the first and to date only Indian state to have an official policy on women, should be required to implement its own suggested measures with particular urgency regarding Nepali women in prostitution, who not only are the frequent victims of harassment and abuse by law enforcement officials, but who also have little understanding of or access to information about their rights in India.

NEPAL'S LAWS

Nepal's constitution, adopted in 1990, its civil code and several specific laws forbid the trafficking and sale of women and children and other forms of slavery and provide for prison sentences of up to twenty years for interstate trafficking and sale of human beings. Article 20 of the Nepali constitution states:

> 1. Traffic in human beings, slavery, serfdom or forced labour in
> any form is prohibited. Any contravention of this provision shall
> be punishable by law.

The constitution is supplemented by a national legal code called the *Muluki Ain*,[22] which contains provisions against interstate and domestic trafficking in human beings. Section 1 of the law governing "traffic in human beings" decrees prison sentences of twenty years for international trafficking cases where the victim has already been sold and sentences of ten years of imprisonment for attempted sale, plus fines equivalent to the amount of the transaction. In cases where the purchaser is found within Nepal's borders, he or she is subject to the same punishment as the seller.[23]

Section 3 of the *Muluki Ain* also forbids slavery and all other "transactions in human beings." Section 2 prohibits the enticement and separation of children under sixteen from their legal guardians. Pimping and solicitation of prostitutes is

---

[22]The *Muluki Ain* was first codified in 1854. It was promulgated anew after the adoption of the 1962 Constitution, has been amended many times since then and remains in effect today.

[23]*Muluki Ain*, "Traffic in Human Beings," (*Jiu Masne Ko)*, Section 1, Amended October 2, 1964, December 19, 1975.

forbidden under Section 5 of a law entitled "Intention to Commit Adultery."[24]
Intercourse with a child under fourteen is considered rape, regardless of consent.[25]

Article 4 of the Traffic in Human Beings (Control) Act of 2043
(1986/1987) expressly forbids the sale of "human beings with any motive; the
transport of "any person abroad with intent of sale," the act of "compel[ling] any
woman to take to prostitution through allurement or enticement, deceit, threats,
intimidation, pressures or otherwise; and "conspiracy for committing any of the
acts mentioned." The act applies the same penalties to these offenses regardless of
whether they are committed inside or outside Nepal's territorial boundaries and
makes no distinction between crimes committed by Nepalis or by foreigners. The
act dictates prison terms of ten to twenty years for trafficking in human beings and,
disturbingly, reverses the burden of proof, requiring the accused in a trafficking
case to disprove the charges.[26]

In 1990, the newly elected government of Nepal ratified the United
Nations Convention on the Rights of the Child. In May 1992, Nepal passed the
Children's Act 2048. The act defines a child as any person under sixteen years of
age and Section 15 states that: "No person shall involve or use any child in an
immoral profession." It also contains a number of provisions designed to prevent
other kinds of sexual exploitation of children including child pornography and

---

[24]*Muluki Ain,* "Intention to Commit Adultery" (*Asaya Karani Ko*), amended
December 19, 1975. Section 5 states: "In cases where a person entices a woman with the
intention of arranging sexual intercourse with himself or with any other person, or
arranges contacts and affairs with prostitutes, he shall be punished with imprisonment for
a term ranging from six months to two years, or with a fine ranging from Rs. 500 to Rs.
6000, or both."

[25]*Muluki Ain,* "On Rape," (*Jabarjasti Kavani Ko*), Section 1, amended December 19,
1975.

[26]The presumption of innocence is a fundamental principle laid down in Article 14(2)
of the ICCPR. Reversing the burden of proof in trafficking cases is therefore a breach of
international law. Note: Trafficking cases are prosecuted by a government prosecutor,
and traffickers retain private attorneys to defend them. This has meant that activists and
human rights lawyers who follow trafficking as an issue of concern have had little access
to court documents or information about the process of on-going legal cases. Likewise,
women who have made complaints against traffickers complained they were not kept
informed about the progress of their cases.

prohibits discrimination between daughters and sons, the use of children for begging, the sale of girl children as religious offerings to temple deities, or for child labor.[27]

FINDINGS OF U.N. SPECIAL RAPPORTEUR

The 1993 report of then U.N. Special Rapporteur on the Sale of Children, Vitit Muntarbhorn, was particularly important in outlining the role of official forces in trafficking and in drawing the link between industrial recruiting, bonded labor and forced prostitution in Nepal, concluding that Nepal's "[l]aw enforcement authorities are often weak, understaffed, undertrained and corrupt..." and that "[t]here is an expansive web of criminality which exploits children and which abuses the open border with India." Muntarbhorn added, "[t]here is still insufficient transfrontier cooperation both to prevent child exploitation and to ensure safe return and rehabilitation of children subsequently."[28] He called for improved law enforcement, investigation and punishment of corrupt officials, better international cooperation on trafficking, including national cooperation with Interpol, and the establishment of national policy bodies to deal with child exploitation.

The report concluded that: "[w]hile the legislative and policy framework to respond to children's rights are in place to some extent in Nepal, there is evidently poor implementation and weak enforcement at the national and local levels," problems aggravated by legal inconsistencies in a variety of Nepali laws and discrepancies between international standards and national law regarding the

---

[27]*The Children's Act 2048; A Bill to Provide for Safeguarding the Interests of Children,* was signed by the king on May 20, 1992. Section 5 prohibits discrimination between sons and daughters, Section 7 forbids torture and cruel treatment, Section 13 prohibits "offering of girl child in the name of God or Goddess," Section 15 states that "Children [shall] not be made involved in immoral professions," and Section 17 provides protections against "engaging in hazardous work."

[28]*Rights of the Child; Sale of children, child prostitution and child pornography, Report submitted by Mr. Vitit Muntarbhorn, Special Rapporteur, in accordance with Commission on Human Rights resolution 1993/82, Addendum, Visit by the Special Rapporteur to Nepal,* pp. 7-8.

age of majority (16 in Nepal, 18 under the Convention on the Rights of the Child). The report noted that legal shortcomings were compounded by a widespread failure to register births, making it difficult to establish the age of Nepali children and child workers and thus to enforce international standards designed to protect them.

The report found that in general legal remedies were not easily accessible to the victims of abuse and that law enforcement lacked both training and the will to confront child exploitation:

> (e) Several laws, such as the Constitution, depend for their implementation upon various ministries and the bureaucracy. This means that, in effect, the rights inherent in such laws are not justiciable; it would be difficult to resort to courts to enforce them. In any case, in view of the physical and mental distance between the majority of the population, who are rural based and often illiterate, on the one hand, and the formal judicial structure, on the other hand, there is a wide gap between availability of legal remedies and genuine accessibility of those remedies.

> (f) Law enforcement authorities are often weak, understaffed, undertrained and corrupt. Interestingly, during the Special Rapporteur's dialogue with the police, the latter complained that the labour laws did not clearly confer upon the police the power to raid illegal factories and that this was within the mandate of the labour inspectors. This type of obfuscation and "burden-shifting" does not bode well for law enforcement and child protection.[29]

These findings correspond with those of Human Rights Watch/Asia. Despite the abundance of legislation aimed at preventing trafficking and other forms of slavery, neither India nor Nepal has adequately enforced existing laws, investigated reports of official complicity in the trafficking industry or prosecuted officials found profiting from the trade. The apparent apathy on the part of both

---

[29] *Rights of the Child; Sale of children, child prostitution and child pornography, Report submitted by Mr. Vitit Muntarbhorn, Special Rapporteur, in accordance with Commission on Human Rights resolution 1993/82, Addendum, Visit by the Special Rapporteur to Nepal,* p.7.

governments, the highly organized nature of trafficking networks which include influential government officials, and the temptation of easy money makes police corruption virtually inevitable.

VI. CONCLUSIONS AND RECOMMENDATIONS

Increased awareness in recent years of violence against women and children has helped focus international attention on the problem of trafficking and forced prostitution. Ratification of the Convention on the Rights of the Child by many countries, the appointment in 1994 of a U.N. special rapporteur on violence against women, and the continuing work of the special rapporteur on the sale of children, child prostitution and child pornography, with mandates to investigate and report on abusive conditions and make recommendations to the governments in question to end abuse, have helped put pressure on the U.N. and its member states to recognize the seriousness of the trafficking problem.[1] But while the reporting of these agents has been accurate and detailed, and some countries have taken steps to curb the involvement of their citizens in trafficking and sexual exploitation, particularly of girls, much more needs to be done to control the trade, address the issue of official complicity, and protect women and girls against victimization.

International attention to trafficking in women first focused on Thailand and its position at the epicenter of a global trafficking industry. The international media did much to raised awareness about the phenomenon of sex tourism in Southeast Asia. U.N. agencies were soon asked to take up the issue of the sex trade in other countries, including Nepal and India, and to recognize the enormity of the domestic sex market. The rapid spread of AIDS in India, the world's second most populous country, has been a crucial factor in this shift of focus. International aid agencies, including UNICEF and UNDP, and agencies concerned with the spread of HIV and AIDS like the World Health Organization, have also acknowledged the issue of trafficking and prostitution in relation to their education and relief efforts.

What has been lacking so far is a well-organized, multilateral effort to control the industry. Despite public acknowledgement of the problem and an Interpol initiative focused specifically on the trafficking of minors, governments have failed to make the control of human smuggling and forced prostitution issues of urgency for regional or global crime control initiatives, and virtually no effort has been made at those levels to address complaints of official involvement in trafficking. Securing state accountability for violations of fundamental human rights is an essential element of human rights protection. India, Nepal and the

---

[1] Vitit Muntarbhorn, who served as U.N. Special Rapporteur on the Sale of Children from 1989, resigned his post in late 1994 citing personal reasons and lack of support from the U.N.

84

international community have an obligation to ensure that states rigorously pursue prosecution of those of its own forces found guilty of complicity with the industry.

TO NEPAL

Human Rights Watch/Asia is deeply concerned that as long as there remains a demand for Nepali girls and women in India's brothels, and a lack of alternative sources of income in Nepal's villages, trafficking in women will flourish as a profitable industry. The government of Nepal has an obligation to do everything in its power to check the trafficking and sale of Nepali women and girls from its territory and to protect them from the human rights violations associated with the industry.

1) Nepal should accede to the international instrument most relevant to the trafficking in women and girls: the Convention for the Suppression of Traffic in Persons and the Exploitation of the Prostitution of Others.

2) The government of Nepal should ensure that all reports of trafficking or attempted trafficking be promptly and thoroughly investigated and that those found guilty are prosecuted. The government of Nepal has a special obligation to investigate reports of official corruption and complicity in the trafficking and sale of persons and should hold all persons alleged to have involvement with the industry to the same legal standards. This includes police officers, government officials and influential private citizens.

3) The quality of law enforcement personnel needs to be improved. Human rights training within the police force should include trafficking issues as a priority. The chain of command and responsibilities of the various levels of the police force need to be clearly articulated, and police at all levels should receive frequent, clearly worded directives indicating their responsibility to investigate and arrest traffickers and warning that police found guilty of taking bribes or profiting from the trafficking industry will be prosecuted. Prosecutions should follow.

4) Local village constabulary in particular need to receive better training, including human rights training, and direction in recognizing and investigating trafficking cases. At present village police are considered dangerously untrained by their superiors and are therefore unable to police their communities effectively. Systems of communication between local police posts and district-level police need to be improved and protections put in place which would allow local constables to resist the pressures of criminal gangs operating in their areas. At present these local stations are frequently remote and unprotected, and local police rely heavily on the good will of area bosses.

5) In accordance with Article 20 of the Convention on the Suppression of Traffic in Persons, the Nepali government should monitor and investigate recruitment networks operating in known trafficking centers such as Nuwakot and Sindhupalchowk, carpet factories in Kathmandu, and border towns "to prevent persons seeking employment, in particular women and children, from being exposed to the danger of prostitution."

6) Nepal should establish of a central registry of missing persons and should have information regarding the status of investigations easily accessible to concerned family members.

7) Negotiations between Nepal and India regarding the status of their shared border should include establishing systems for monitoring the trafficking in women and girls and investigating and prosecuting the traffickers to the fullest extent of the law.

8) The government of Nepal should ensure that no trafficking victims repatriated from India or any other country is subjected to arrest, detention, or compulsory medical testing on return to Nepal. The system of shuttling Nepali women from police station to police station and holding returnees in detention until parents or guardians retrieve them is unacceptable and can be viewed as arbitrary detention. The practice of compelling women to undergo HIV testing in detention is equally unacceptable and leads to stigmatization.

TO INDIA

The demand for Nepali girls and women in India's brothels drives the trafficking from Nepal. This demand is fueled by a fear of AIDS and the tastes of the consumer and is made possible by the active support of Indian police. It is essential therefore that India take immediate steps to curb this demand.

1) The government of India should move to reform its prostitution and trafficking laws to ensure they are non-discriminatory and in line with international human rights standards, particularly those designed to protect the victims of trafficking. While Human Rights Watch takes no position on prostitution *per se*, we consider the disproportionate application of those articles of ITPPA and the Bombay Police Act which allow police to arrest persons for public prostitution but not brothel owners, pimps or traffickers to be discriminatory. At the same time, individuals forced into prostitution should be exempt from any punishment or involuntary remand to reform institutions.

2) India and Nepal's five-hundred-mile open border makes it essential that both countries give priority to strict monitoring efforts to guard against the

trafficking in women and girls, including the inspection of vehicles. Special training should be given to law enforcement officials at the border in the problem of trafficking and their obligation to protect trafficking victims and investigate those who engage in such abuse.

3) The government of India should actively investigate and prosecute all those involved in trafficking and brothel operations, with particular attention to its own police and officials who receive payoffs or protection money from brothel owners and/or agents, patronize illegal brothels, have financial holdings in, collect rent from, or in any other way are complicit in the operations of such brothels.

Investigations of official involvement must be both thorough and impartial. A hotline might be established to receive allegations of official involvement, with safeguards established for the protection of witnesses. Information could then be turned over to a commission of inquiry for investigation, with the record of the proceedings public to the extent that witness security permits. Prosecutions of officials, including members of the police, should take place in civilian courts in proceedings that are open to the public.

4) Officials found guilty of involvement in trafficking and/or brothel operations, or of failing to enforce the law with respect to those operations, should be prosecuted to the fullest extent of the law. Suspensions, transfers or public apologies for complicit law enforcement officials is not sufficient.

5) All laws which can lead to the prosecution of all others involved in trafficking and brothel operations, including recruiters, agents, brothel owners and pimps, should be strictly enforced. Brothel owners, for example, are responsible for forcible procurement of women, outlawed under the IPTTA, each time that they compel one of their workers to have sex with a client. Clients who engage in sex with children below the age of sixteen could and should be arrested for rape under the Indian penal code.

6) Any case involving the detention of a Nepali woman or girl following a raid on a brothel should be given particular attention with a view toward the speedy release of anyone found to be a trafficking victim. If the status of a woman or girl as a trafficking victim is not clear and she is arrested, the Indian government should ensure that her civil rights are fully protected, including that she understands the nature of the charges against her, has access to an interpreter and legal counsel and is tried without undue delay before a fair and impartial tribunal, with the right of appeal thereafter. Special efforts should be made to protect women from having to decide between lengthy detentions or being bailed out by pimps or brothel owners claiming to be family members.

7) To protect Nepali women and girls against abuse by Indian police, the Indian government should ensure the presence of women police officers in all

places of detention. The government should also investigate any report of extortion and sexual abuse in detention and prosecute those responsible to the fullest extent of the law. The rights of detainees to be protected against abuse and the procedures for submitting complaints against officials should be available in the Nepali language in Indian jails and be explained fully to detainees on arrival.

8) The Indian government should ensure that all detention facilities conform fully to the U.N. Standard Minimum Rules for the Treatment of Prisoners.

9) The Indian government should ensure that arrangements with the Nepali government for the safe return of trafficking victims ensure the protections guaranteed by the Convention on the Suppression of Traffic in Persons. In the case of indigent women, it should bear the cost of their repatriation to the border and arrange for Nepal to bear any additional costs, a process that is now *ad hoc* at best. The agreement with the Nepali government should contain guarantees for the legal protection and privacy of women and girls returning from India. Under no circumstances should the Indian government agree to selective and discriminatory repatriation on the basis of the ethnic or racial background of the women and girls concerned. Because of the danger posed by organized crime, and the social stigmatization associated with prostitution, both governments should protect the women's right to privacy by prohibiting access to confidential or biographical information about the women. The Indian and Nepali press should also agree on an ethical code that would restrict the use of names or identifiable photographs of these women from appearing in the print or broadcast media unless the women in question have specifically consented.

10) The Indian government should ensure that all HIV testing of prostitutes is of a non-compulsory nature and that when it is undertaken with the informed consent of the women and girls, those tested should be informed of the results if they so request.

TO THE INTERNATIONAL COMMUNITY

The Secretary-General of the United Nations and the United Nations High Commissioner for Human Rights should ensure that all United Nations agencies pay particular attention to the issue of trafficking in women and develop programs and strategies designed to curb that abuse and encourage accountability. U.N. agencies that have AIDS programs in India and Nepal, including WHO, UNDP and UNICEF should use these programs to focus attention on the human rights implications of the AIDS pandemic, including the role of official forces in the trafficking of women and the dangers of discrimination against victims of the disease.

Because the Nepali women and girls in the brothels are trapped in virtual slavery, unable to negotiate any aspect of their situation, or count on police protection, information on AIDS is admittedly of limited practical use. Nonetheless, it is one of their only remaining lines of defense against contracting and transmitting the AIDS virus. AIDS education for the Nepali women will help them assert some control over their lives by informing their decisions about marriage and children if they return to their home villages. And information for the general public, including potential male customers, may hopefully deter some from high-risk behavior. The World Health Organization's Global Program on AIDS lists public information and education as critical elements of the fight against AIDS.[2]

Trafficking of women is an increasingly global industry. The Beijing Women's Conference in September 1995 provides an ideal forum in which to promote the issue of trafficking in women as a primary human rights concern worldwide. The members of SAARC should also be encouraged to make trafficking in women and children a regional priority at their periodic meetings.

Influential countries such as Japan, which have good relations with both India and Nepal and which have ratified the relevant international instruments related to trafficking, should urge the latter two countries to ratify or accede to those instruments and to work out an agreement on repatriation and protection of trafficking victims.

Other Asian countries and donor countries in other regions should encourage India and Nepal to adopt the recommendations outlined above and should use every opportunity to raise the problem of trafficking both publicly, at international meetings, congressional or parliamentary hearings, and in press conferences; and privately, in meetings with relevant officials. They should work to develop programs and strategies for bilateral and multilateral aid programs to India and Nepal that would make funds available for certain kinds of training, education, information dissemination and legal reform programs related to trafficking, but would also make some assistance programs conditional on evidence of effective prosecution of officials, brothel owners, agents and pimps.

---

[2] WHO-GPA has noted that "the keystone of HIV prevention is information and education, as HIV transmission can be prevented through informed and responsible behavior." "Report of an International Consultation on AIDS and Human Rights," United Nations Centre for Human Rights and the World Health Organization's Global Program on AIDS, Geneva, 26-28 July, 1989, p. 33.

Interpol, the Nepali police, the Indian police, and the South Asian Association for Regional Cooperation should cooperate to identify international trafficking networks that exploit women and children. India and Nepal should have a special police force mandated to deal with trafficking. Communication and joint training sessions between border personnel should be improved and encouraged, as should extradition agreements and information exchanges.